Australia
Visions of a Continent

Australia
Visions of a Continent

This edition published in 2015 by New Holland Publishers Pty Ltd
London • Sydney • Auckland

Unit 009, The Chandlery 50 Westminster Bridge Road London SE1 7QY UK
1/66 Gibbes Street Chatswood NSW 2067 Australia
218 Lake Road Northcote Auckland New Zealand

www.newhollandpublishers.com

Copyright © 2015 New Holland Publishers Pty Ltd
Copyright © 2015 in text: New Holland Publishers Pty Ltd
Copyright © 2015 in images: Shaen Adey/New Holland Image Library, with the exception of the photographers and/or their agents listed below.

Photographic credits
All photographs © Shaen Abey/NHIL with the exception of the following:
Vicki Hastrich/NHIL: p87 (bottom); Anthony Johnson/NHIL: 66, 148-49, 150–51, 156; Jiri Lochman/Lochman Transparencies: 108; NHIL: 54, 81 (left); courtesy of Phillip Island Penguin Reserve: p42 (bottom); Nick Rains/NHIL: , 20 (bottom), 24.

All rights reserved. No part of this publication may be reproduced, stored in a retrieval system or transmitted, in any form or by any means, electronic, mechanical, photocopying, recording or otherwise, without the prior written permission of the publishers and copyright holders.

A record of this book is held at the British Library and the National Library of Australia.

ISBN 9781742576268

Managing Director: Fiona Schultz
Project Editor: Angela Sutherland
Designer: Peter Guo
Production Director: Olga Dementiev
Printer: Toppan Leefung Printing Ltd (China)

10 9 8 7 6 5 4 3 2 1

Keep up with New Holland Publishers on Facebook
www.facebook.com/NewHollandPublishers

Page 1: Colourful bathing huts on Brighton Beach, south of Melbourne.
Pages 2–3: The Sydney Opera House at sunset.

CONTENTS

INTRODUCTION 6

NEW SOUTH WALES 8

AUSTRALIAN CAPITAL TERRITORY 32

VICTORIA 36

TASMANIA 60

SOUTH AUSTRALIA 80

WESTERN AUSTRALIA 90

NORTHERN TERRITORY 119

QUEENSLAND 136

Timor Sea
Melville Is.
Gurig N.P.
Bathurst Is.
DARWIN
Kakadu N.P.
Arnhem Land
Litchfield N.P.
Katherine
Nitmiluk N.P.
Drysdale River N.P.
Kimberley Region
Lake Argyle
King Leopold Ranges
Durack Range
Victoria
Purnululu N.P.
Gregory N.P.
Daly Waters
INDIAN OCEAN
Broome
Fitzroy
Tanami Desert
Northern Territory
Barkly Tableland
Tennant Creek
Devils Marbles
Port Hedland
De Grey
Great Sandy Desert
Millstream-Chichester N.P.
Chichester Range
Hamersley Range
Pilbara
Karijini N.P.
Rudall River N.P.
Cape Range N.P.
Ashburton
Newman
Lake Mackay
Lake Disappointment
Gibson Desert
West MacDonnell N.P.
MacDonnell Ranges
Alice Springs
Lake Neale
Finke Gorge N.P.
Carnarvon
Monkey Mia
Little Sandy Desert
Petermann Ranges
Uluru
Kata Tjuta
Uluru–Kata Tjuta N.P.
Western Australia
Murchison
Lake Carnegie
Witjira N.P.
Simpson Desert
Simpson Desert N.P.
Simpson Desert Regional Reserve
Sturts Stony Desert
Kalbarri N.P.
Great Victoria Desert
South Australia
Lake Eyre N.P.
Cooper Creek
Coober Pedy
Lake Barlee
Lake Moore
Nambung N.P.
Kalgoorlie–Boulder
Nullarbor Plain
Nullarbor Reserve
Yellabinna Reserve
Lake Torrens
Woomera
Lake Frome
PERTH
Swan
Rottnest Is.
Fremantle
Wave Rock
Norseman
Lake Cowan
Nullarbor N.P.
Ceduna
Lake Gairdner
Port Augusta
Flinders Ranges
Flinders Ranges N.P.
Broken Hill
Cape Arid N.P.
Esperance
Stirling Range N.P.
Eyre Peninsula
Leeuwin–Naturaliste N.P.
Walpole–Nornalup N.P.
Fitzgerald River N.P.
Cape Le Grand N.P.
Great Australian Bight
Port Lincoln
Barossa Valley
ADELAIDE
Flinders Chase
Kangaroo Is.
Gulf of Carpentaria
Jardine River N.P.
Cape York Peninsula
Great Dividing Range
Great Barrier Reef
Lizard Is.
Lakefield N.P.
Cape Tribulation N.P.
Daintree N.P.
Green Is.
Atherton Tableland
Kuranda
Cairns
Lawn Hill N.P.
Flinders
Hinchinbrook Is. N.P.
Magnetic Is. N.P.
Burdekin
Townsville
Whitsunday Islands
Hamilton Is.
Airlie Beach
Mount Isa
Mackay
Diamantina
Diamantina N.P.
Longreach
Rockhampton
Lady Musgrave Is.
Carnarvon N.P.
Bundaberg
Fraser Is.
Queensland
Noosa Heads
Sunshine Coast
BRISBANE
Gold Coast
Surfers Paradise
Sturt N.P.
New South Wales
Grafton
Oxley Wild Rivers N.P.
Murray–Sunset N.P.
Mungo N.P.
Wollemi N.P.
Newcastle
Ku-ring-gai Chase N.P.
Katoomba
Blue Mountains N.P.
SYDNEY
Wollongong
Southern Highlands
A.C.T.
CANBERRA
Murray
Snowy Mtns
Kosciuszko N.P.
Grampians (Gariwerd) N.P.
Victoria
Ballarat
Alpine N.P.
Mount Gambier
MELBOURNE
Dandenong Ranges
Croajingolong N.P.
Snowy River N.P.
Port Campbell N.P.
Great Ocean Road
Wilsons Promontory N.P.
SOUTH PACIFIC OCEAN
Great Barrier Reef Marine Park
Coral Sea
Tasman Sea
Cradle Mtn–Lake St Clair N.P.
Flinders Is.
Tasmania
Launceston
Strahan
Macquarie Harbour
Freycinet N.P.
HOBART
Franklin–Gordon Wild Rivers N.P.
Port Arthur
Southwest N.P.
SOUTHERN OCEAN
N

INTRODUCTION

Covering an area of over 7,500,000 square kilometres, the vast island continent of Australia encompasses unique flora and fauna, cosmopolitan cities and a wealth of scenic splendour. Divided into six states and two territories, it is a country with something for everyone, from the lush, primeval rainforest of the Daintree to the harsh, unrelenting deserts of the outback, from the underwater kaleidoscope of the Great Barrier Reef—the world's largest coral structure—to the haunting beauty of Uluru—the world's largest monolith.

This rich diversity is continued in the population. First inhabited by Aboriginal people and then settled as a penal colony by the British, Australia today is home to an eclectic mix of cultures, with recent Asian immigration having swelled the ranks of the earlier European arrivals. Cities such as Sydney and Melbourne with their Chinatowns, Thai restaurants, and Greek and Italian quarters vividly reflect the changing face of modern Australia and, with nearly 90 per cent of the population living in the urban areas of the eastern, southern and south-western coasts, it is a face with which most Australians are increasingly familiar.

But it is the land and its wildlife for which the country is best known. Australia is one of the oldest continents and has remained free of major geological activity for the past 80 million years. As a result of this stability and the continent's geographical isolation, a strange and often unique fauna was able to develop in relative safety, giving rise to, among others, the koalas and kangaroos that have come to symbolise Australia for the international visitor. The floral kingdom is no less spectacular—the several thousand species of wildflower that blossom after the rains in Western Australia form one of the richest plant communities in the world.

For the traveller to Australia, there is much to see and do. New South Wales proclaims itself the Premier State and as its capital Sydney — home to both the Opera House and Harbour Bridge—has hosted global events such as the 2000 Olympics, it is certainly at the forefront of Australian endeavour. The federal capital, Canberra, nestles in the Australian Capital Territory, while further south lie the green fields of Victoria, the tree-lined boulevards of Melbourne, and the breathtaking vistas and tortured rock formations of the Great Ocean Road. South Australia is the state of arts and culture. The biennial Adelaide Festival is a celebration of drama, music, literature and dance, while the Barossa Valley produces wines of international standing. Smallest of the states, Tasmania is known for its historic sites and forested wilderness—an adventure lover's paradise! In stark contrast is Western Australia, occupying one-third of Australia's landmass. Much of the land is arid and inhospitable, dotted with mysterious formations such as the limestone Pinnacles of Nambung National Park and offering a wealth of dramatic scenery. Visitors can also explore the wonders of the Northern Territory—the wetlands of Kakadu National Park, the frontier town of Alice Springs, and the glowing rocks of Uluru and Rata Tjuta. And finally, Queensland invites one to relax and enjoy the 'sunshine' lifestyle of sand, surf and glorious tropical islands.

Left: The Australian continent stretches for over 3600 kilometres from north to south and for over 4000 kilometres from east to west.

Above: Internationally famed icons of Sydney—the breathtaking Opera House and Harbour Bridge.

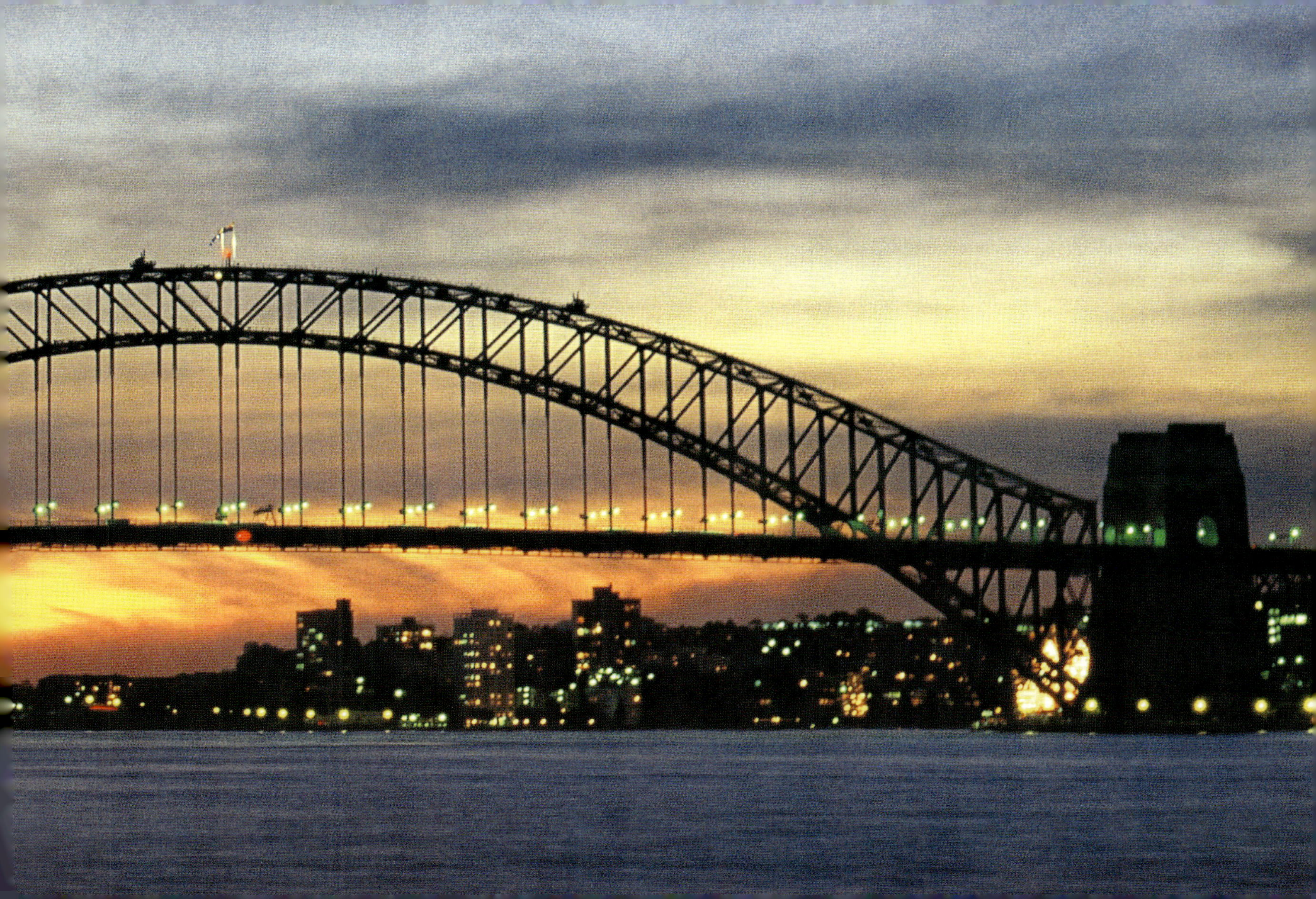

Above: Fireworks light up the harbour in a spectacular New Year's Eve display.

Above centre: Luna Park for family fun.

Above right: Late night patrons flock to Harry's Cafe de Wheels.

Right: Darling Harbour's dining and shopping hub is abuzz with activity day and night.

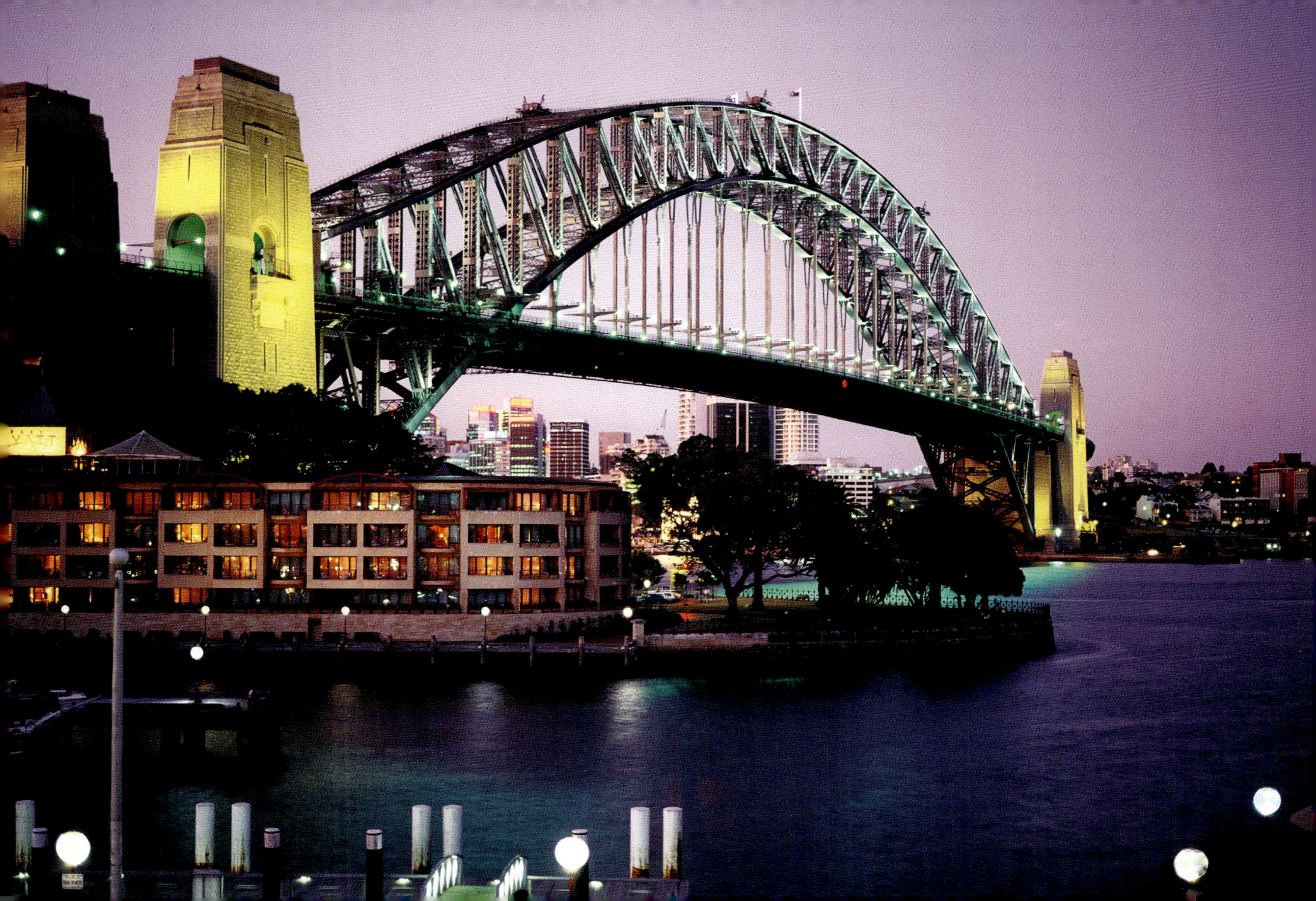

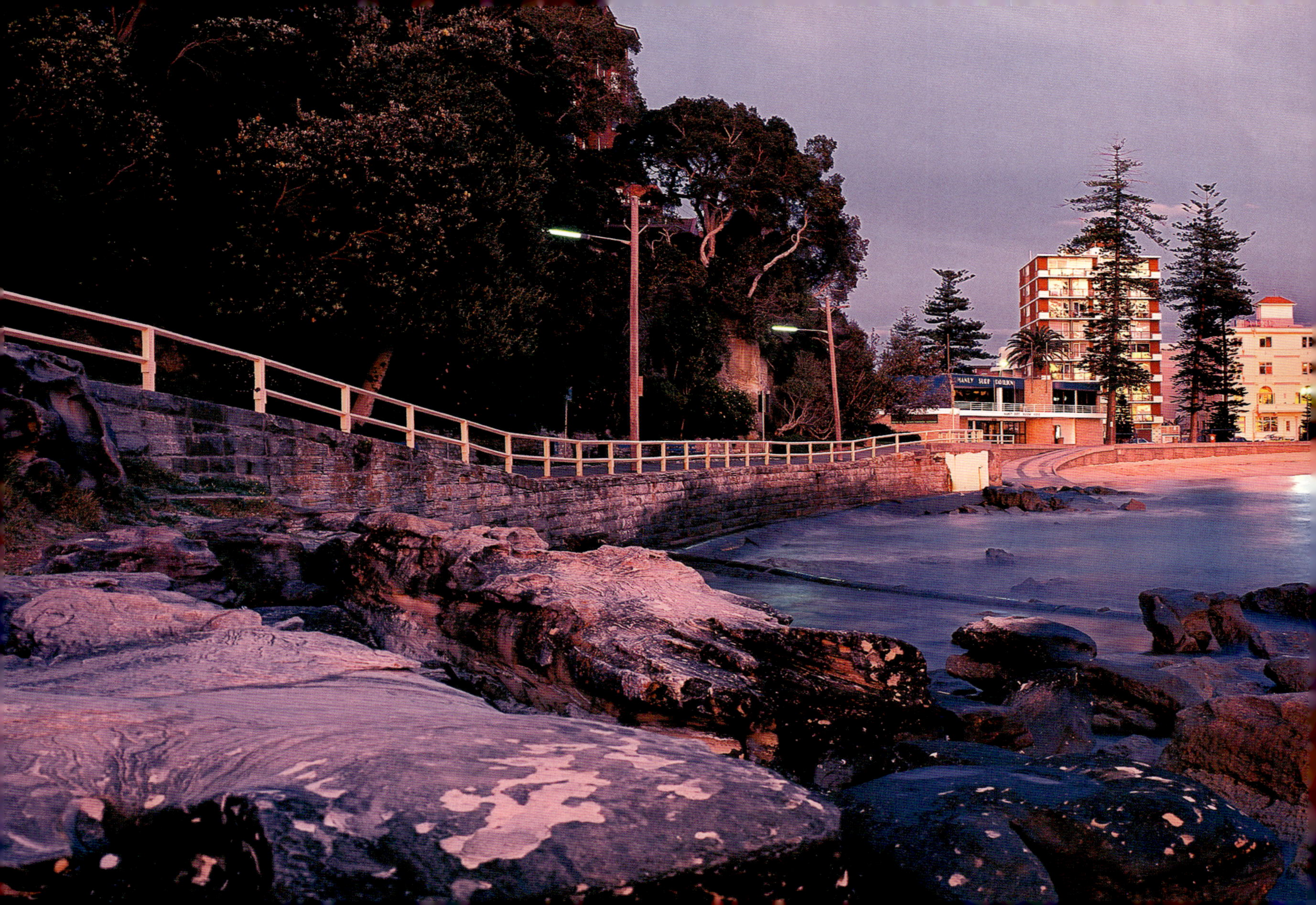

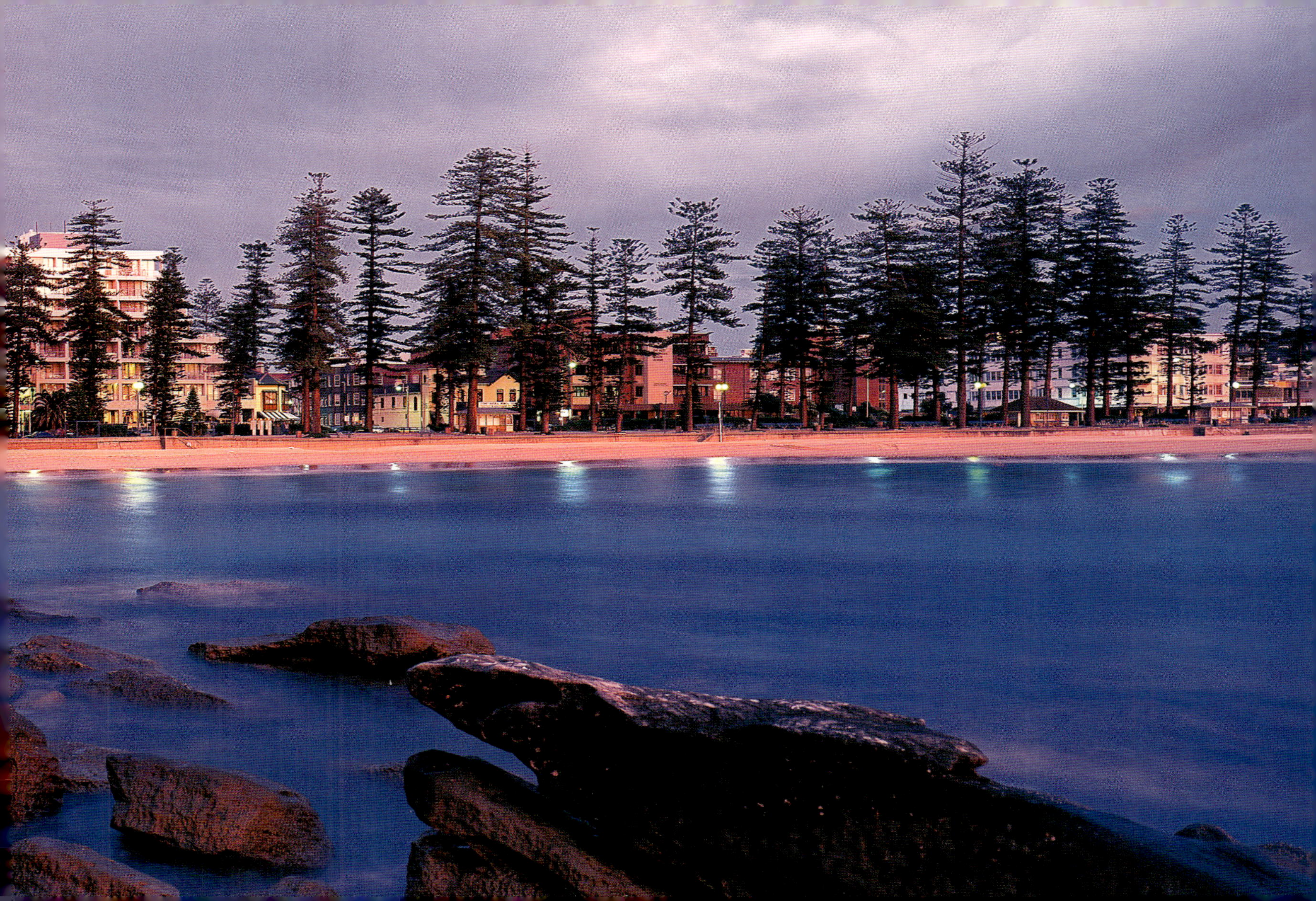

Page 12–13: popular Manly beach.

Left: The Strand shopping arcade has been selling fine wares for generations.

Right: Once Sydney's produce market, the beautifully restored Queen Victoria Building is now an upmarket shopping centre.

Boats race on Sydney Harbour.

The grand finale on New Year's Eve is a spray of light off the Harbour Bridge.

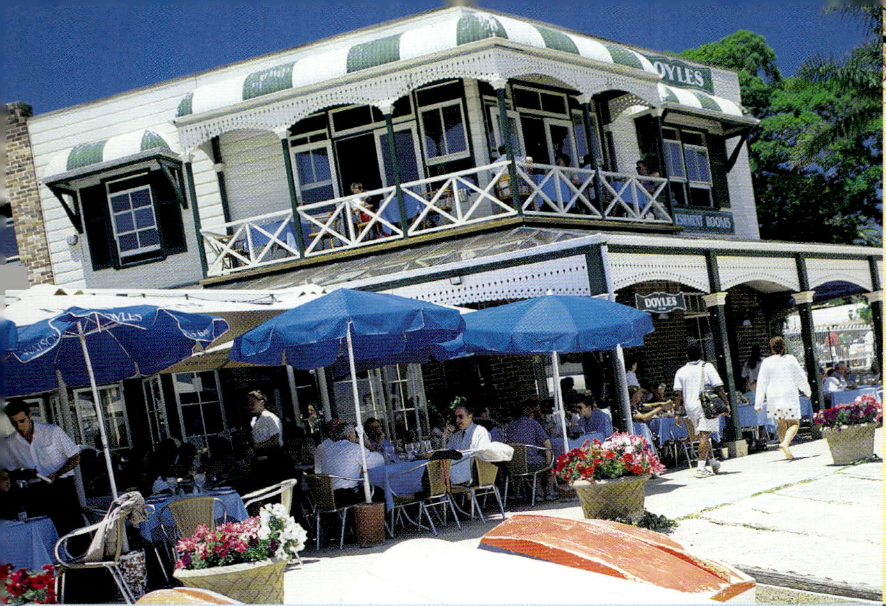
DOYLES
DOYLES

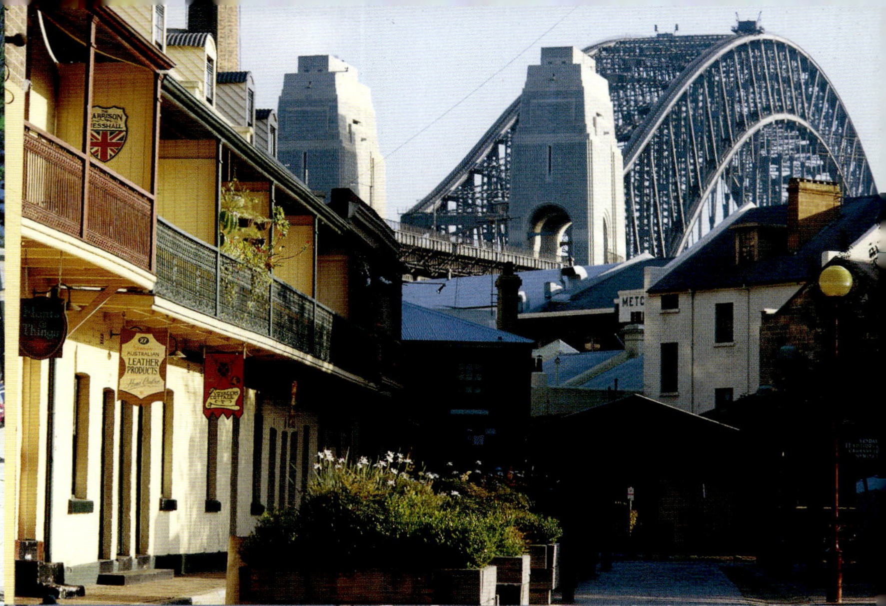
AUSTRALIAN
LEATHER
PRODUCTS

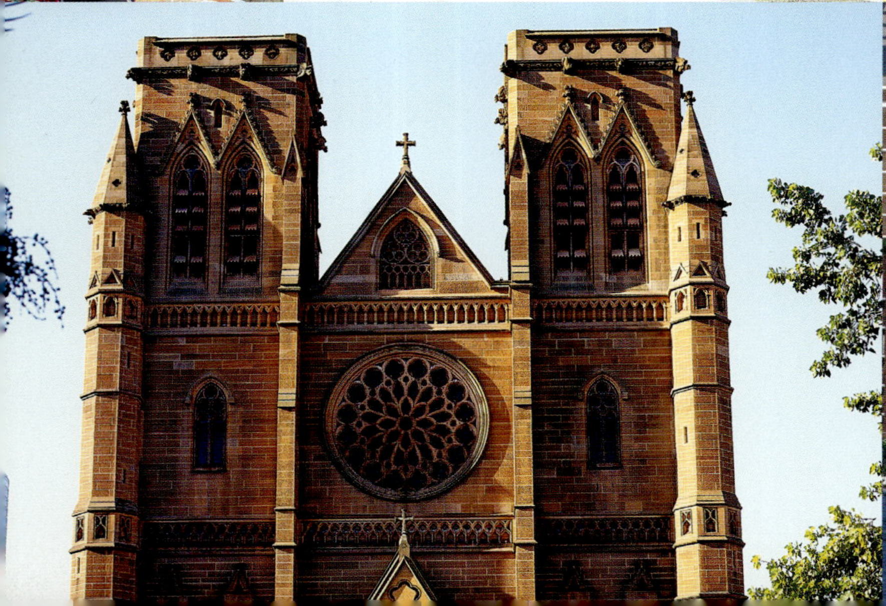

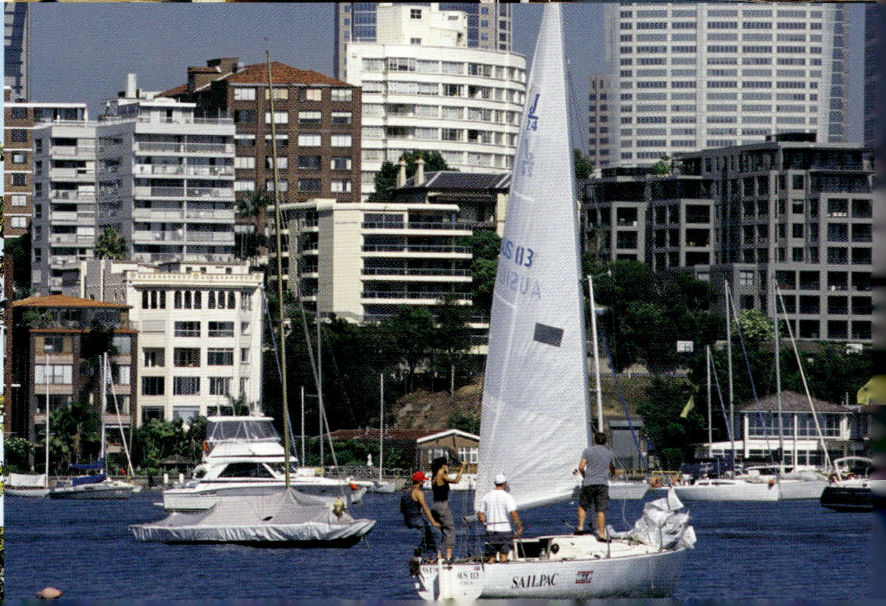
SAILPAC

The famous Icebergs Baths have been a landmark at Bondi Beach for over 100 years.

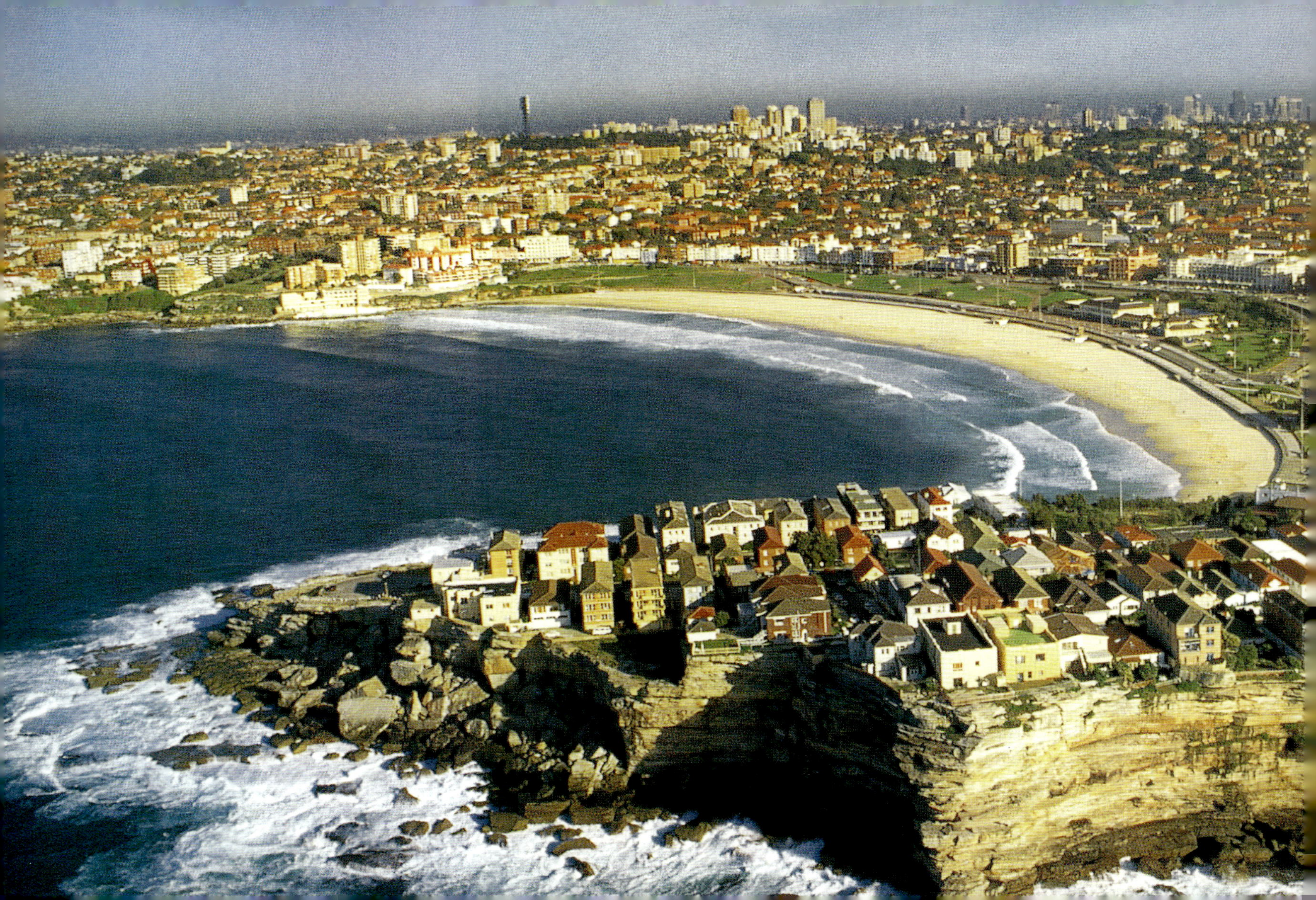

Left and above: Bondi Beach is Australia's most famous stretch of sand. Whether surfing or simply strolling along the shore and cafe-lined esplanade, Bondi's appeal is inescapable.

Lifesavers compete with other surf clubs to stay in top form.

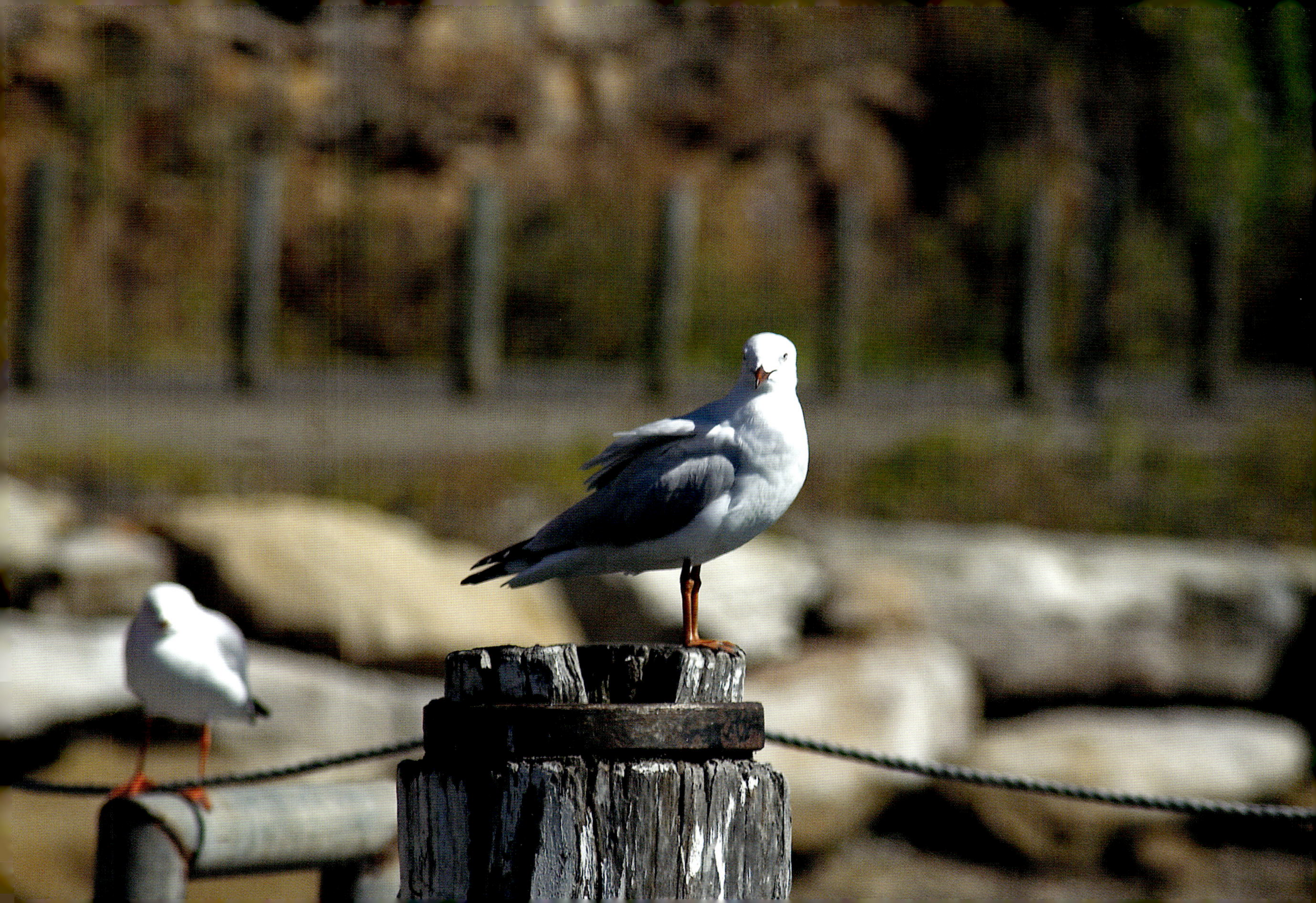

Above and right: Vines were established in the Hunter Valley in 1858 and it has become one of Australia's best known wine-producing areas. Many of the vineyards offer cellar tastings.

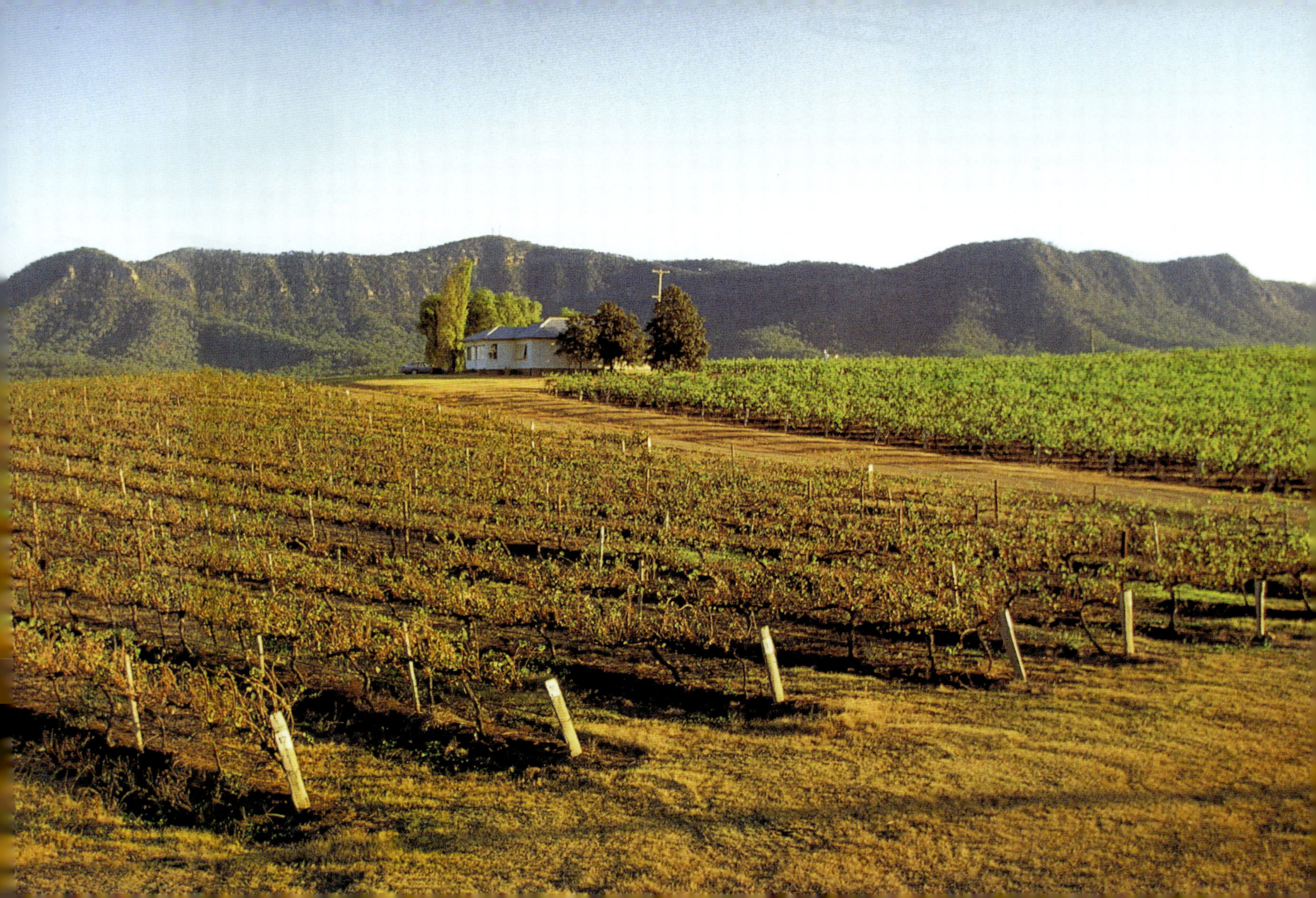

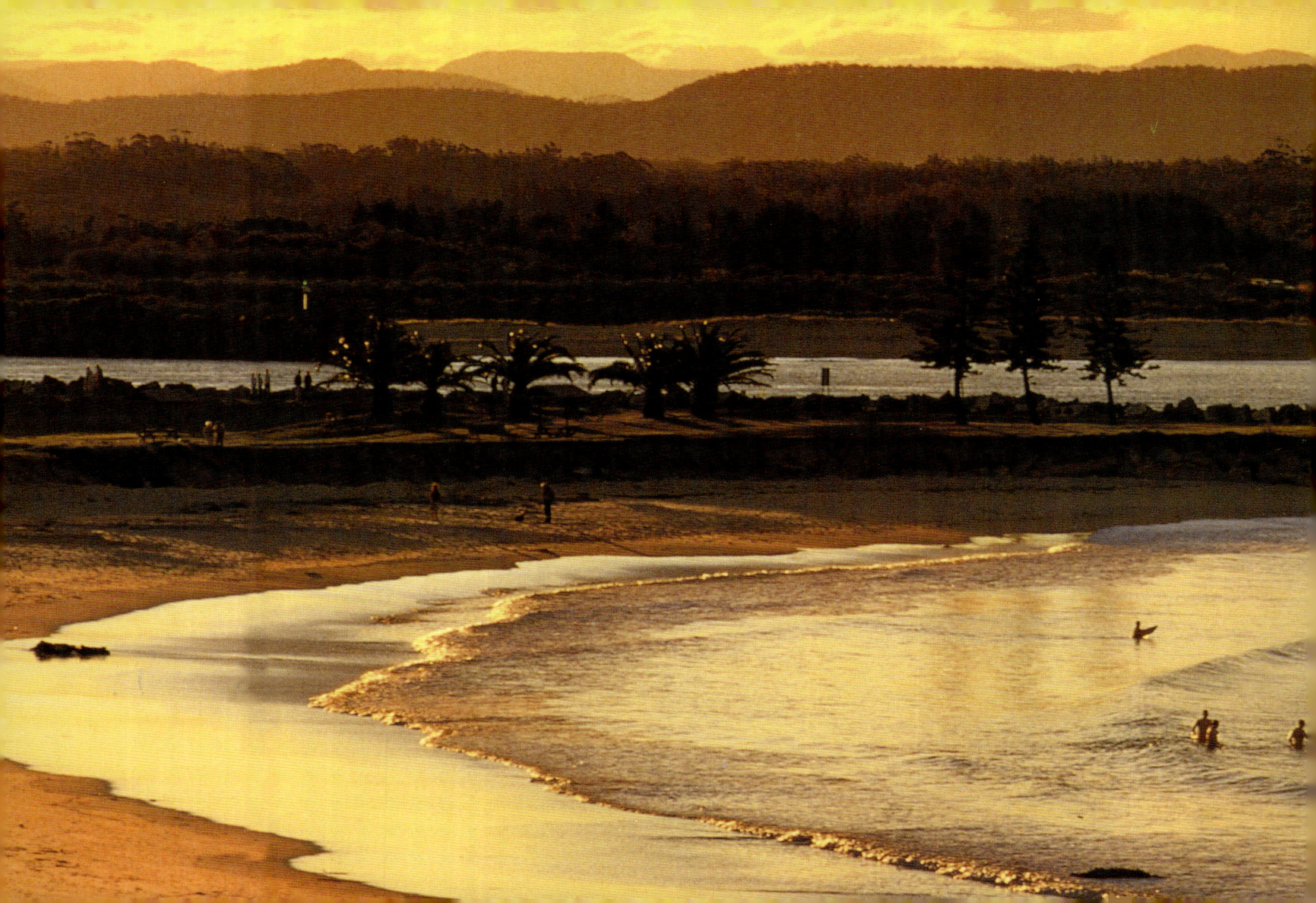

Above: Situated on the far north coast, Byron Bay is one of New South Wales' most well-known holiday destinations. The lighthouse at Cape Byron marks the most easterly point of the Australian mainland.

Left: The coastal town of Port Macquarie lies north of Sydney and is a popular tourist and fishing location.

Lithgow's zig-zag railway was a 19th century engineeringf feat.

The blue haze which gives the Blue Mountains their name is supposedly created by light filteing through the vapour given off by the eucalypt forests.

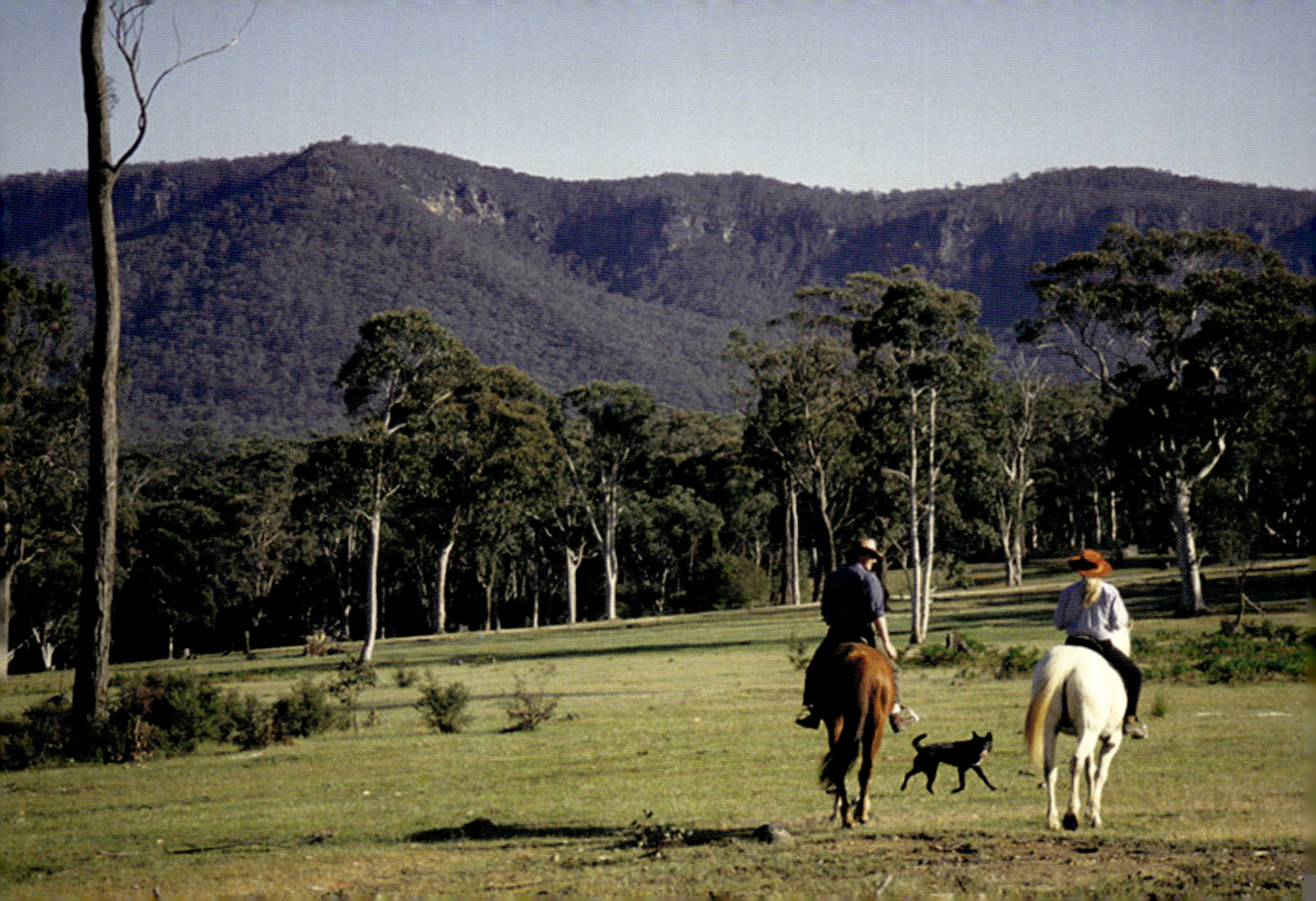

Perisher Valley in Kosciuszko National Park is one of Australia's most popular skiing destinations.

The National Library.

Parliament House.

The War Memorial is both a museum and shrine. Opened in 1941, it was designed to resemble a Byzantine church.

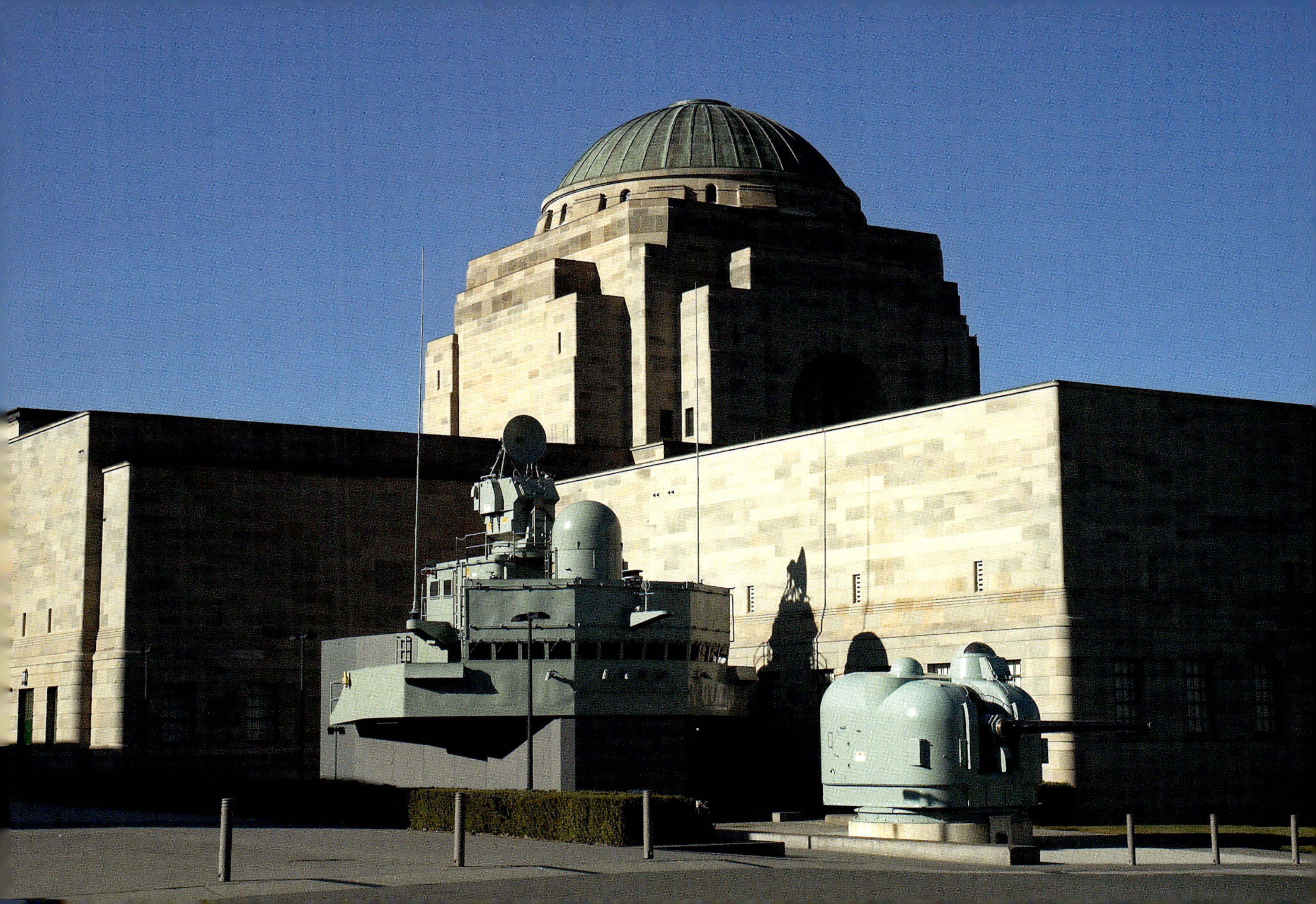

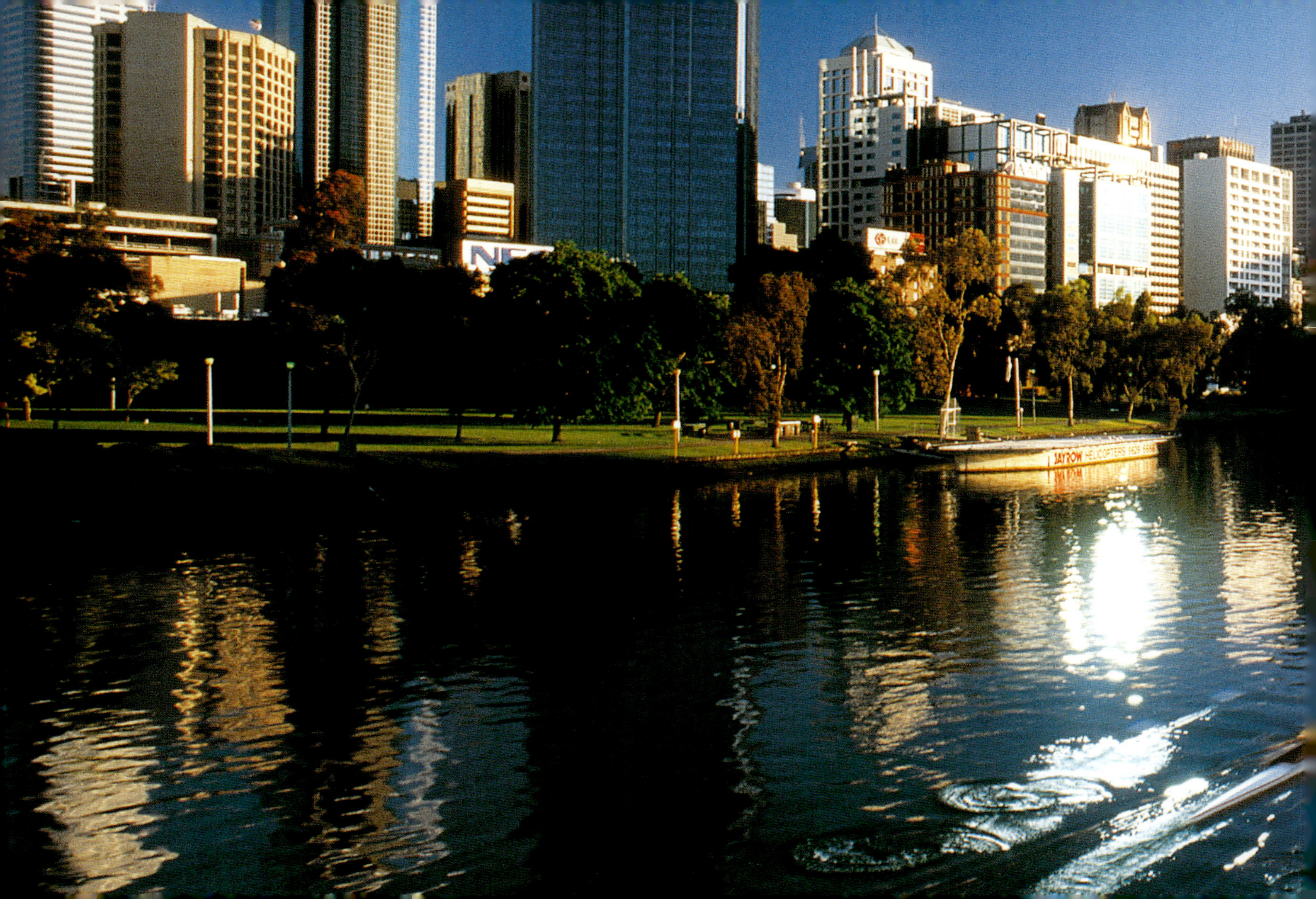
JAYROW HELICOPTERS

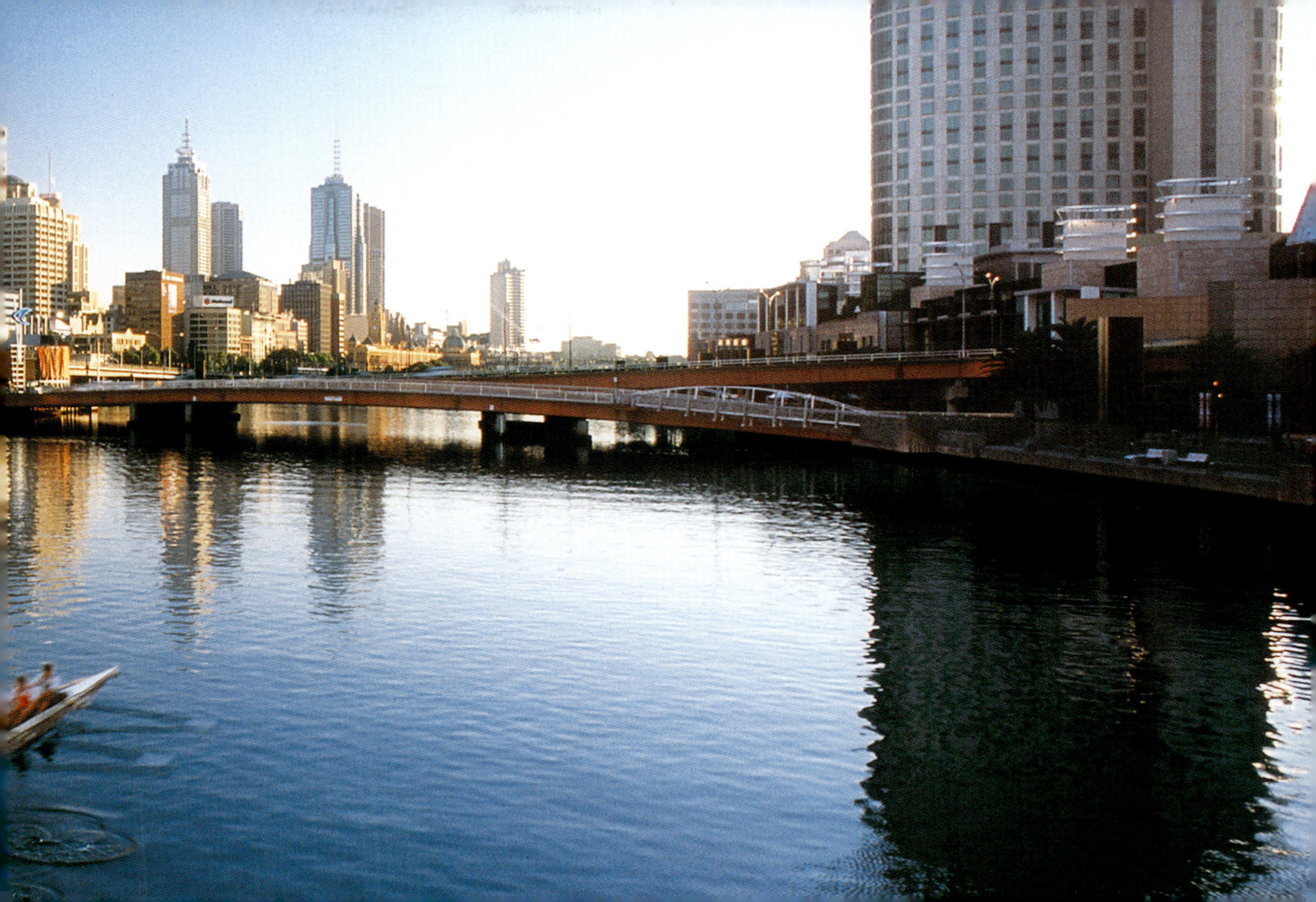

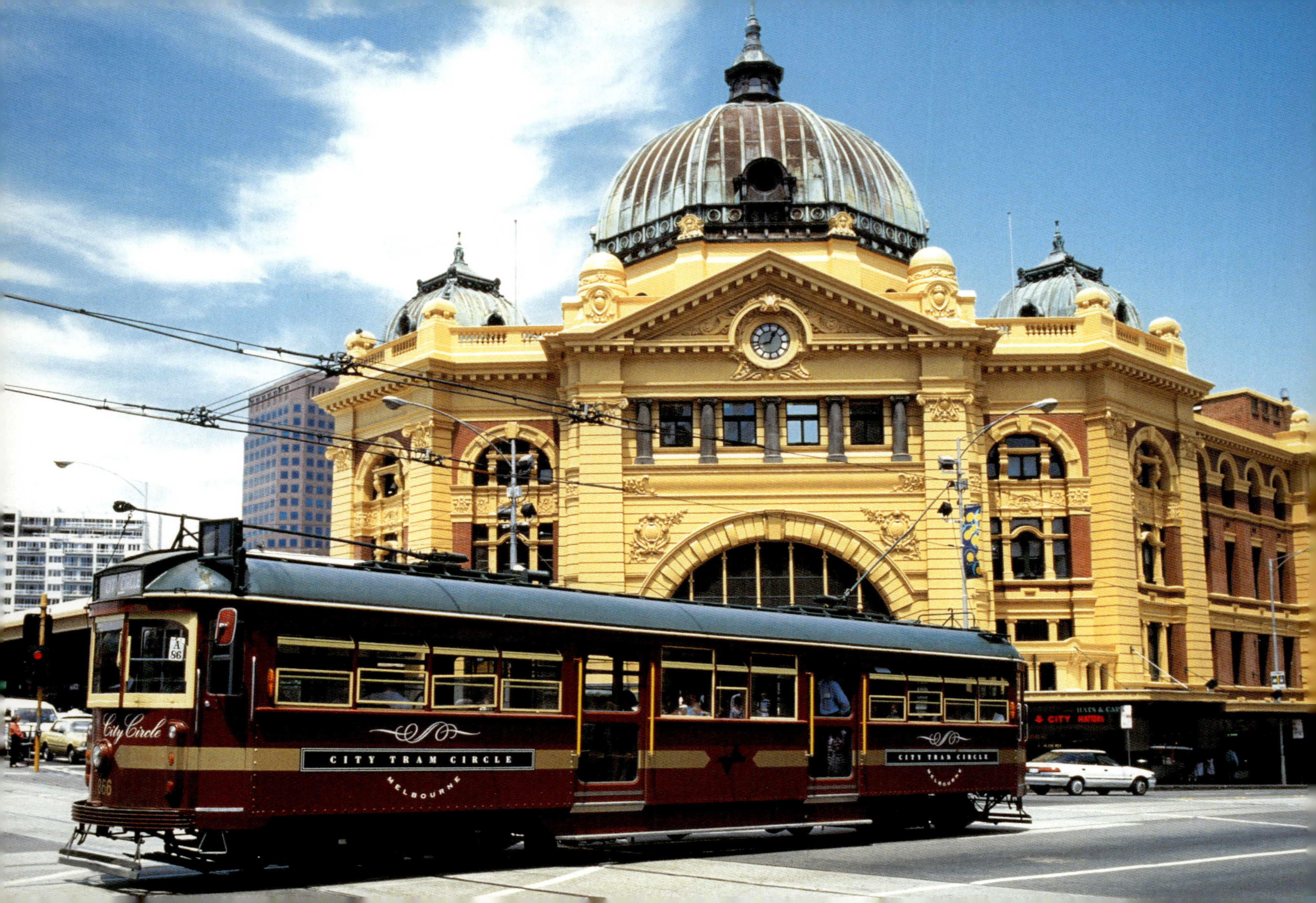
City Circle
CITY TRAM CIRCLE
MELBOURNE

Melbourne's Flinders Street Station is the city's central rail hub.

Federation Square.

Melbourne Exhibition Centre.

Above and top: The Little Penguins of Phillip Island come ashore every night under cover of darkness to return to their rookeries. A visitors centre caters to the large number of tourists who come to watch this penguin 'parade'.

Right: The town of Cowes on Phillip Island attracts holidaymakers to its beach and pier.

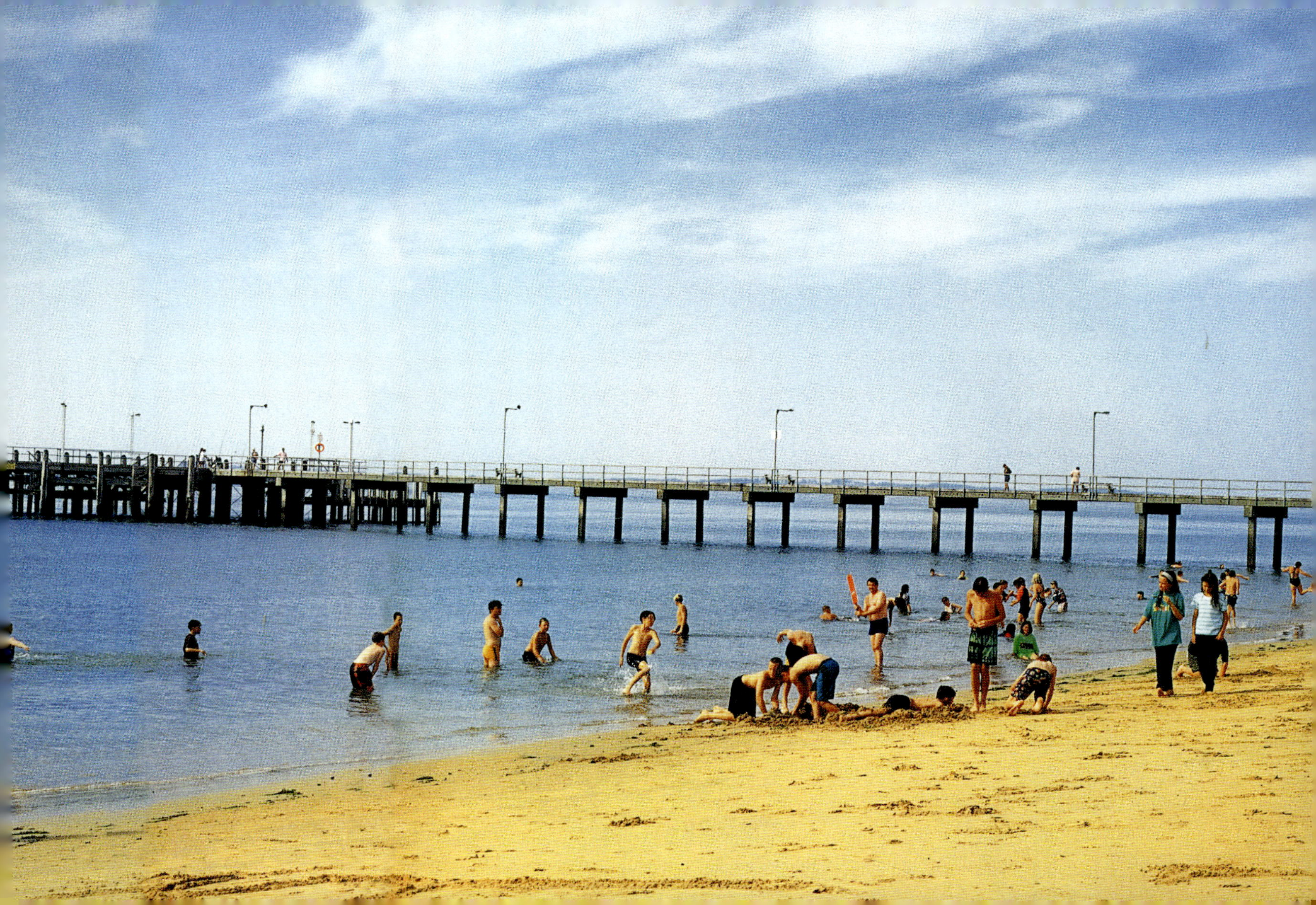

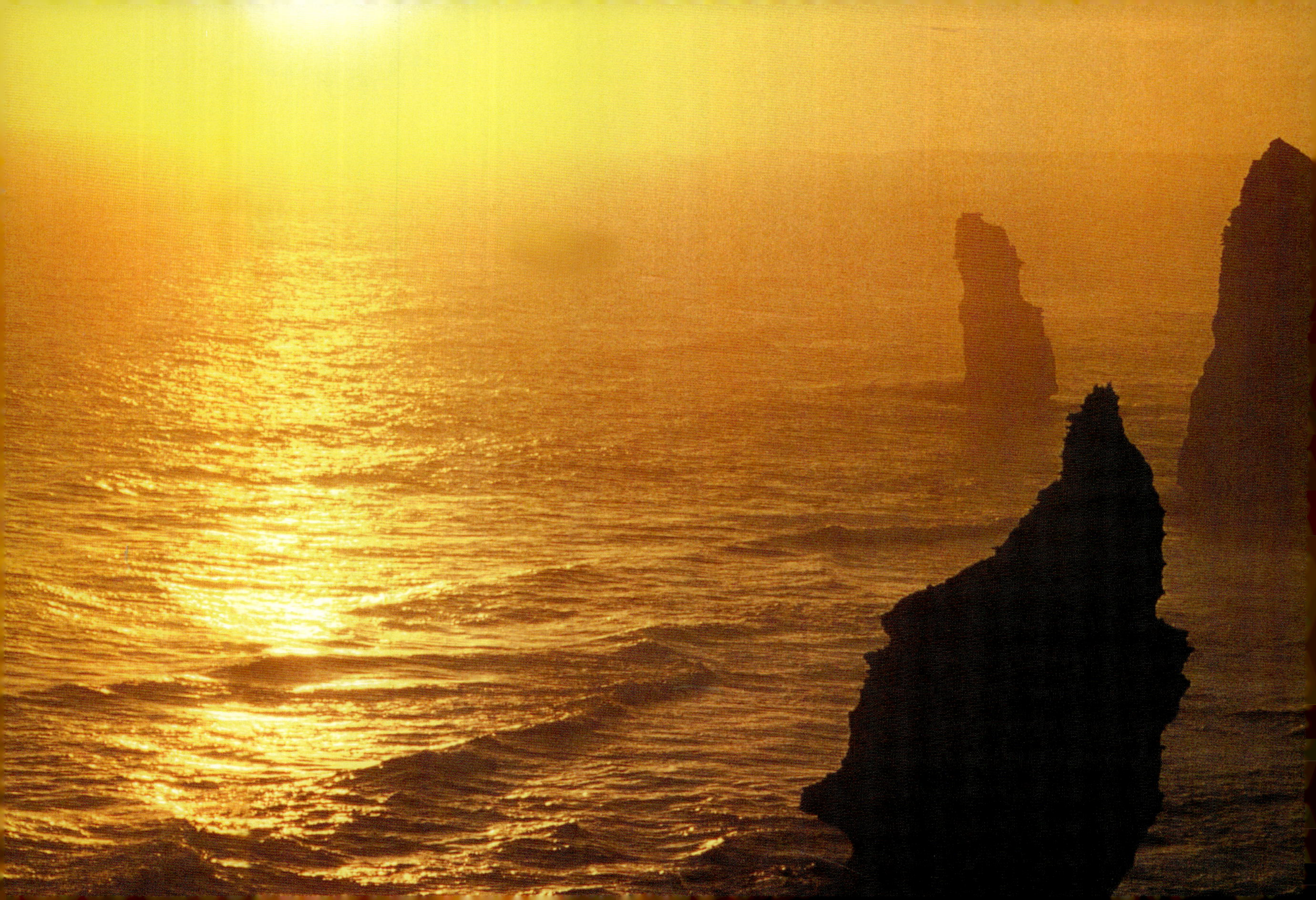

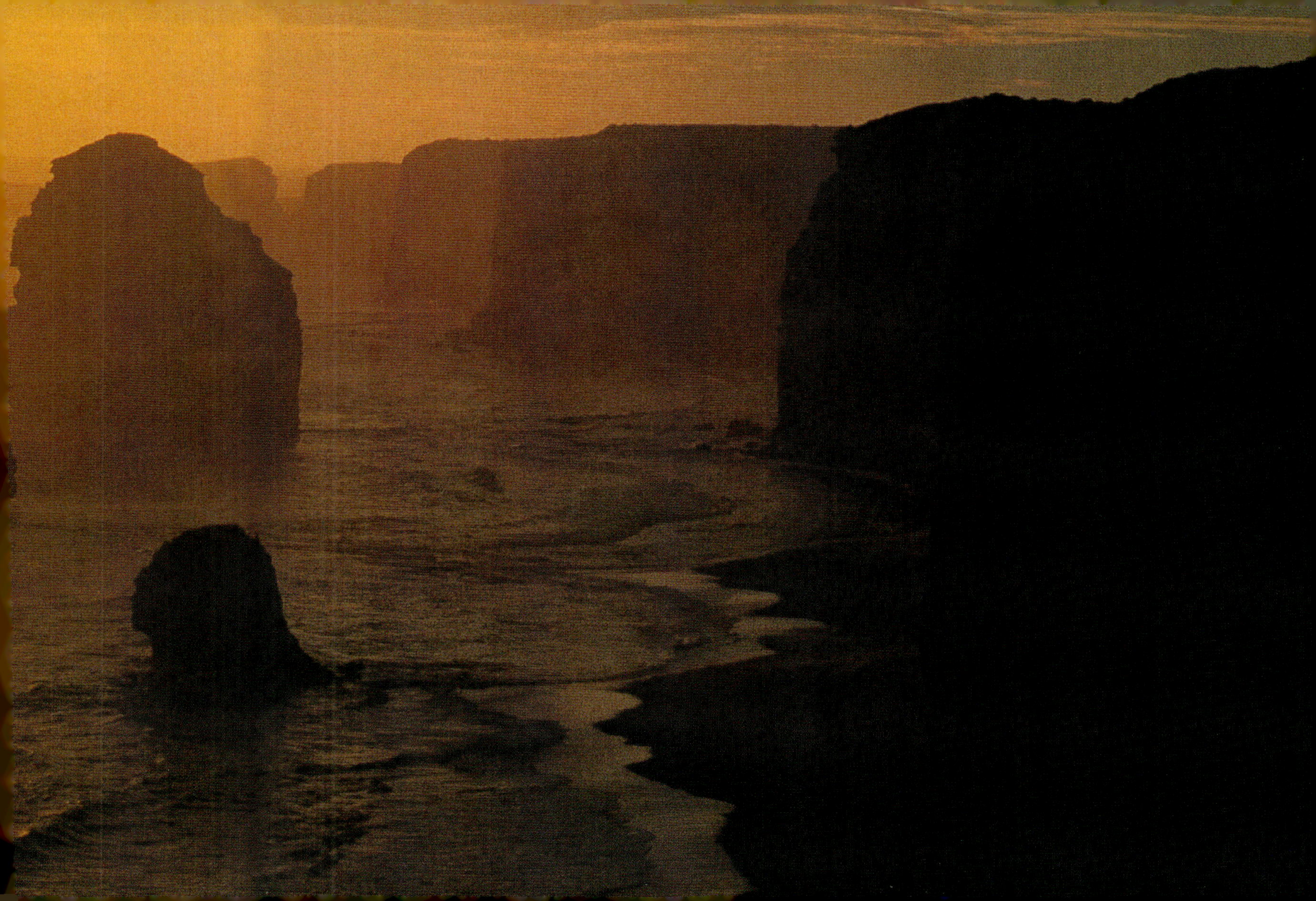

Victoria's rugged coastline boasts dramatic formations such as the Twelve Apostles—stone pillars that have been eroded over the centuries into tortured forms.

The Twelve Apostles form a collection of limestone stacks nestled together just off the Great Ocean Road.

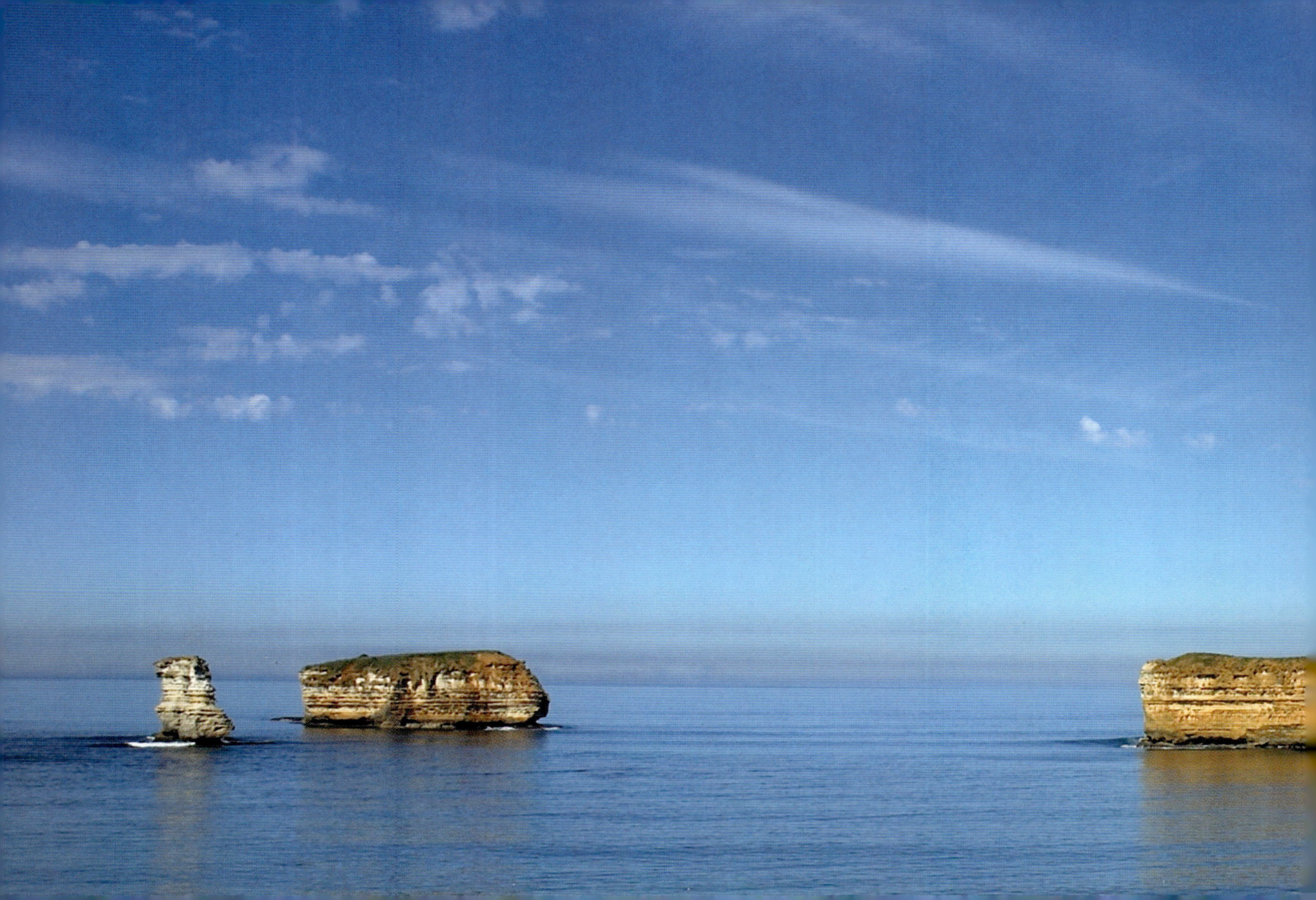

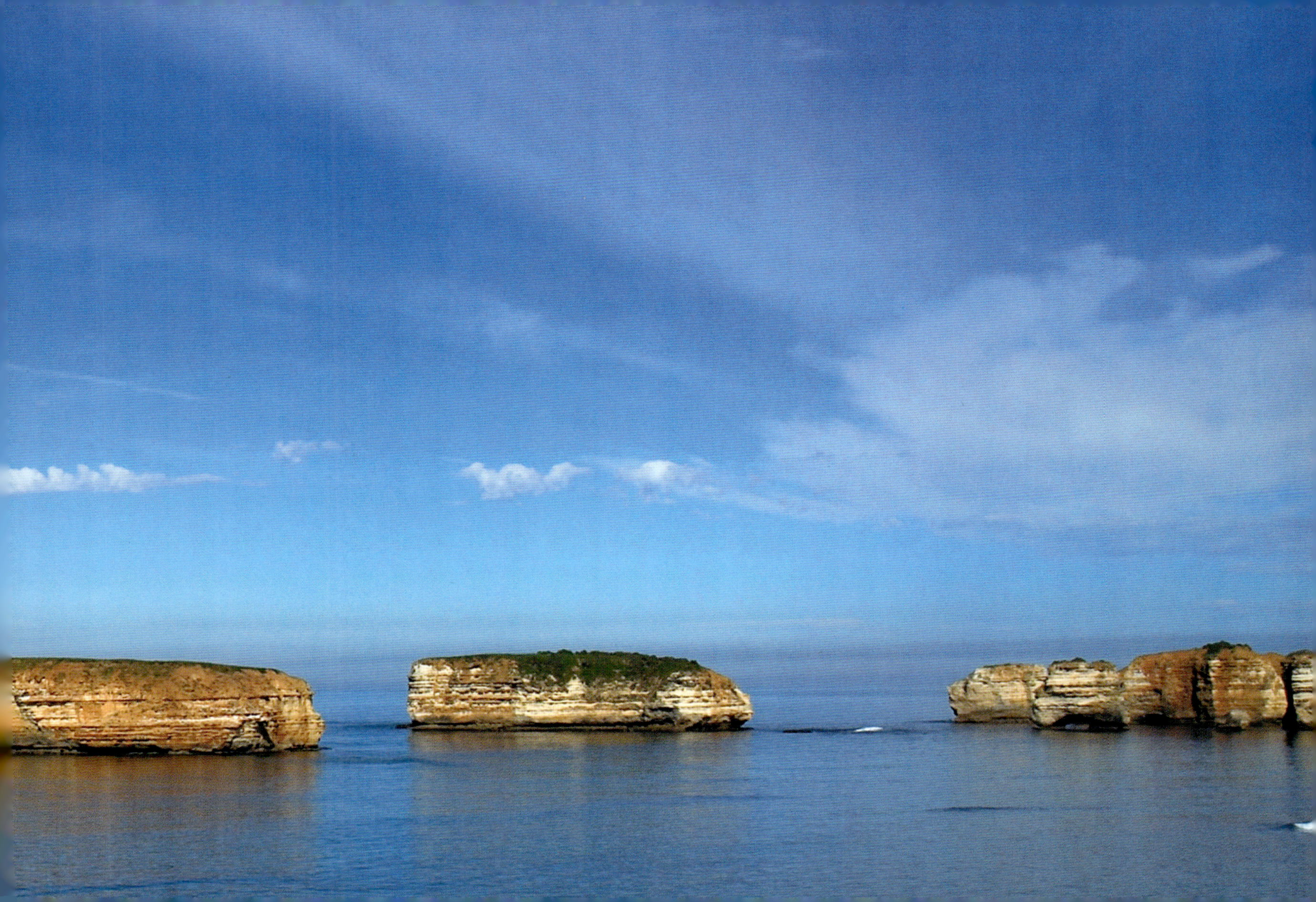

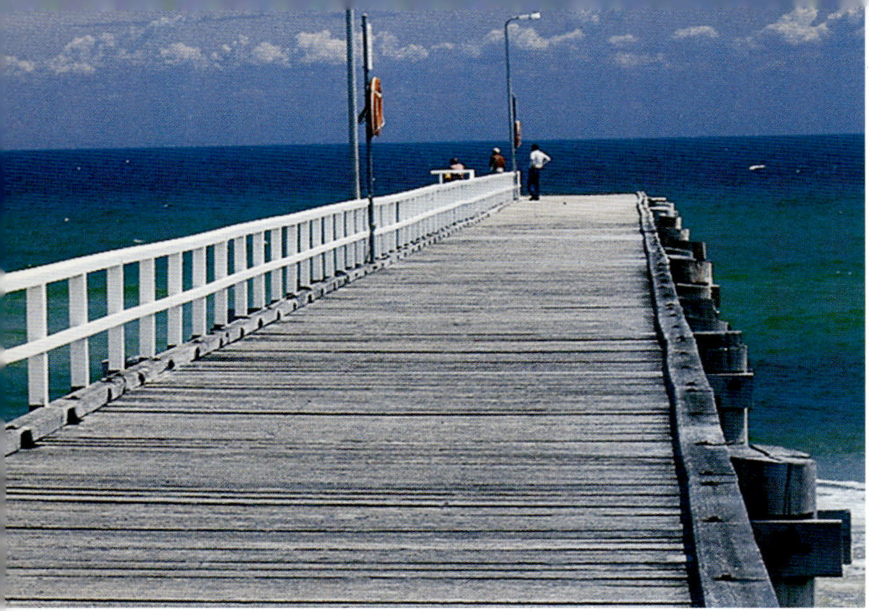
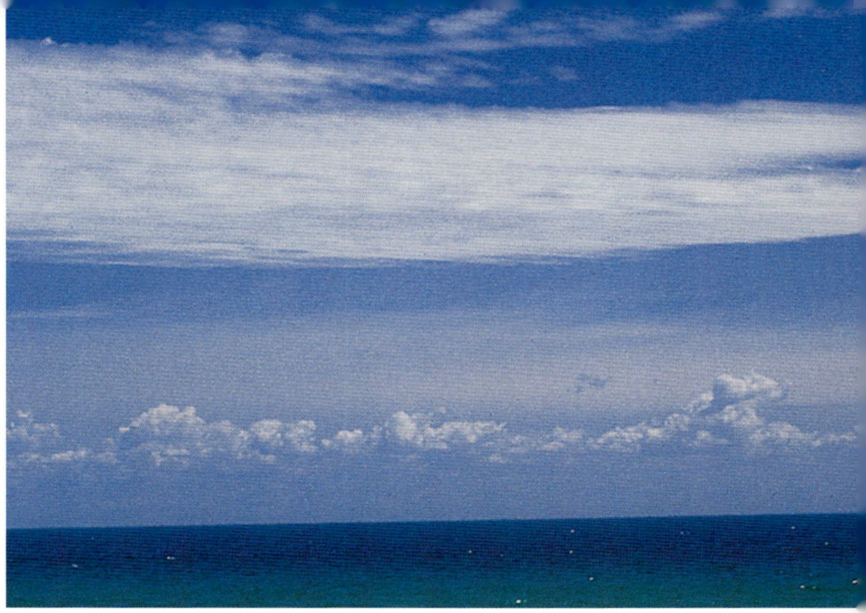
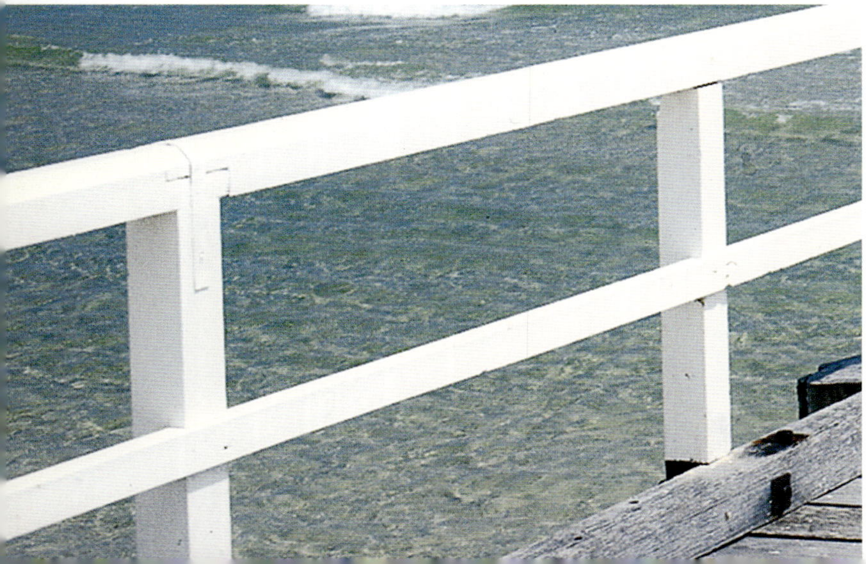
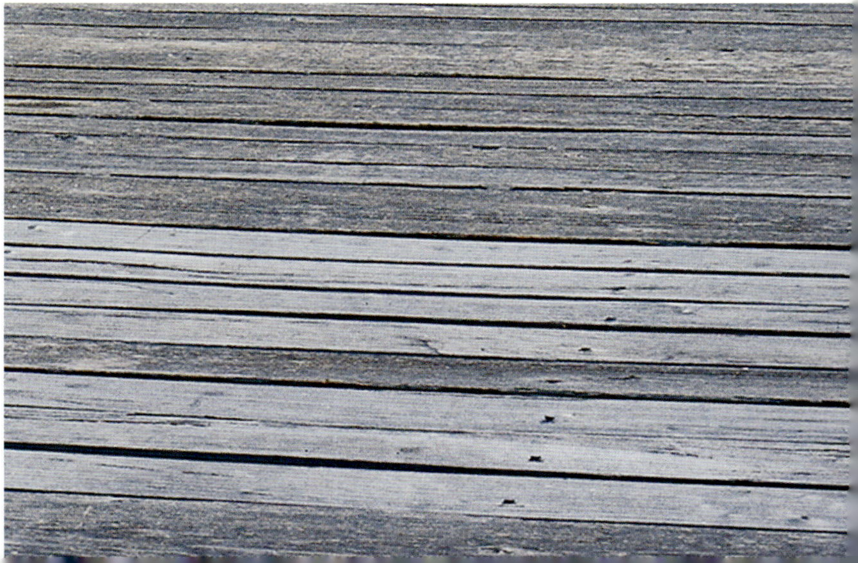

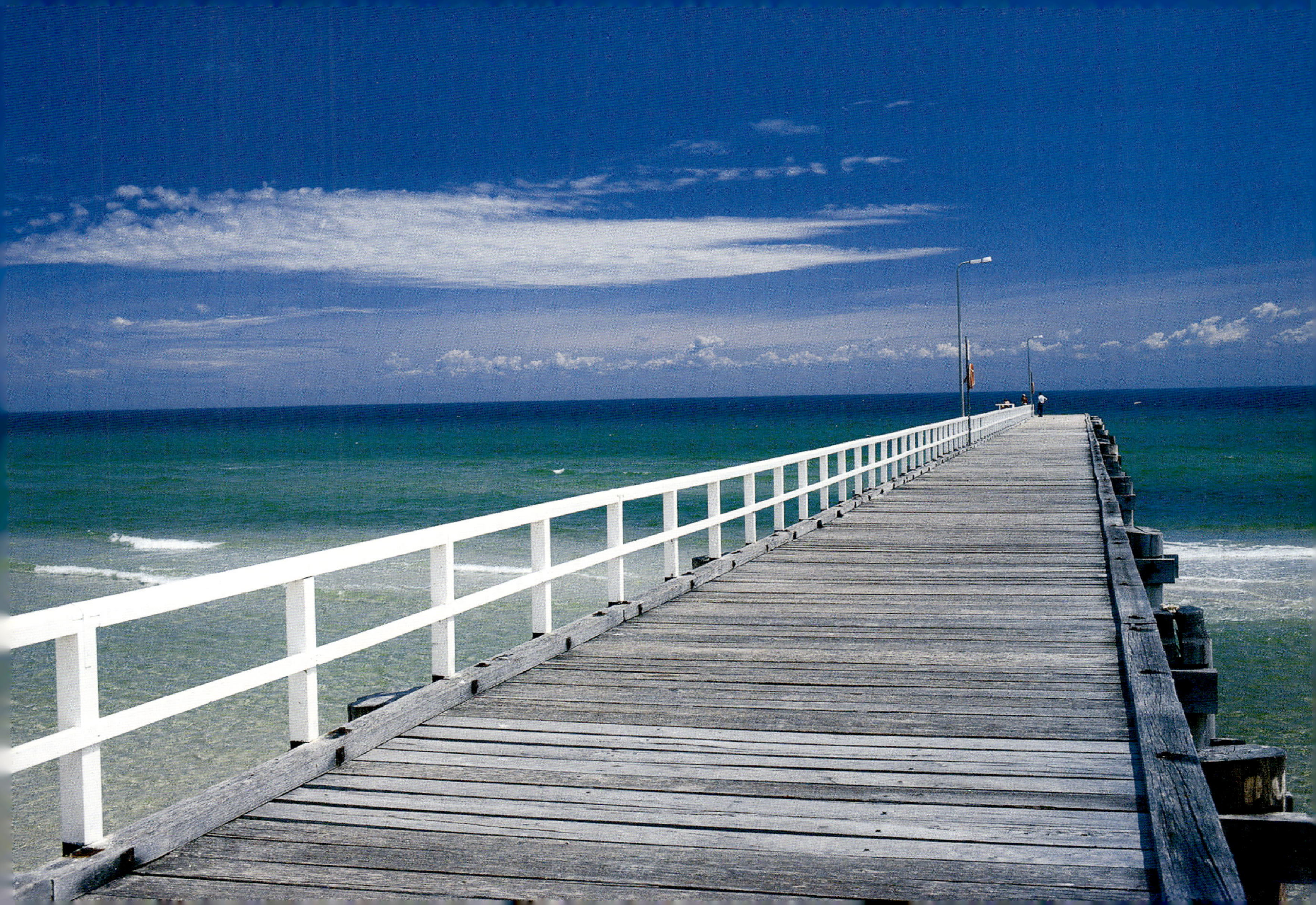

The Ozone Hotel at Queenscliff.

Castlemaine in central Victoria was originally a thriving gold mining town.

Above: Puffing Billy is a popular attraction for visitors to the Dandenong Ranges. The restored steam train travels from Belgrave to Emerald Lake each day.

Right: The farmlands of the Yarra Valley form a striking contrast to the lush forest that covers the nearby Dandenongs.

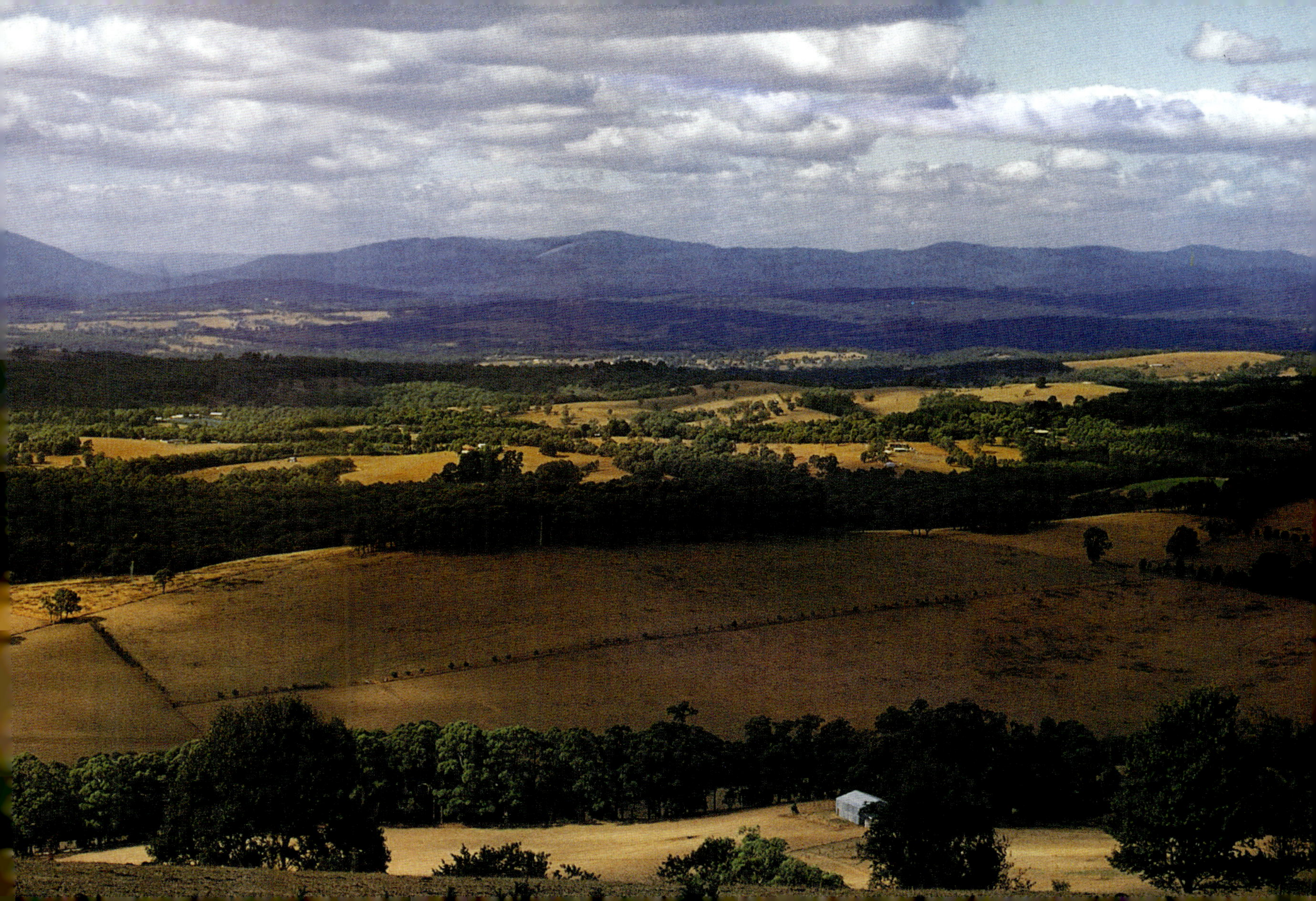

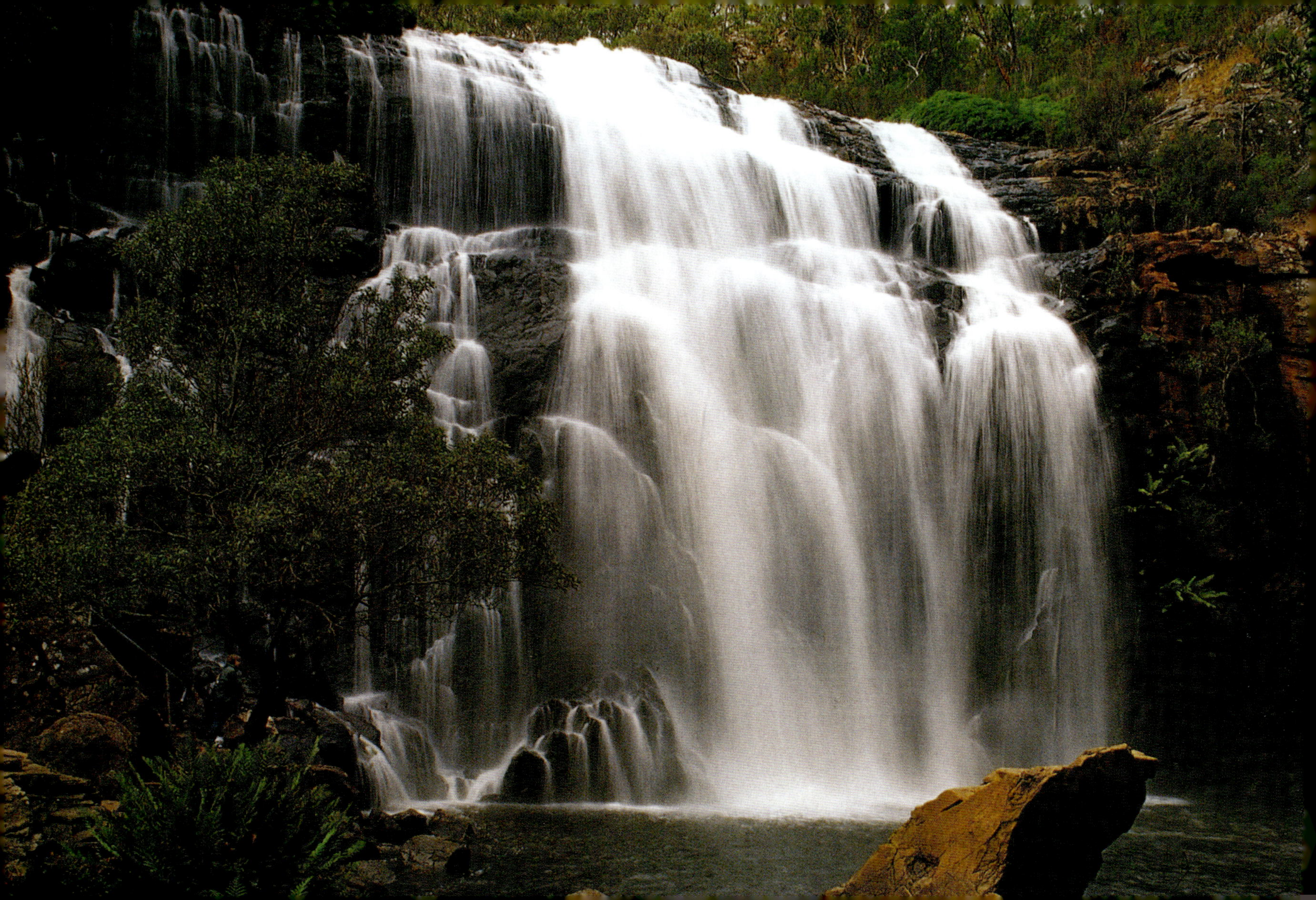

Left: MacKenzie Falls are one of four waterfalls formed as the MacKenzie River plunges over the Great Dividing Range's escarpment.

Right: The Grampians (Gariwerd) National Park encompasses a region of rugged sandstone peaks, rocky overhangs and rich forests.

CLARKE BROTHERS
WHOLESALE & FAMILY
GROCERS
C.SPENCER
T. MURPHY.
JEWELLER
NOW WORKING
GOLD, SILVER & PRECIOUS GEMS

Above: Displaying life as it was during the time of the early settlers, Tyntyndyer Homestead near Swan Hill is now a National Trust building.

Top: Grapes are put out to dry in Mildura, far north-west Victoria. The raisins produced in the region are an important Australian export.

Left: Sovereign Hill, near Ballarat, is a recreation of a 19th-century goldrush town.

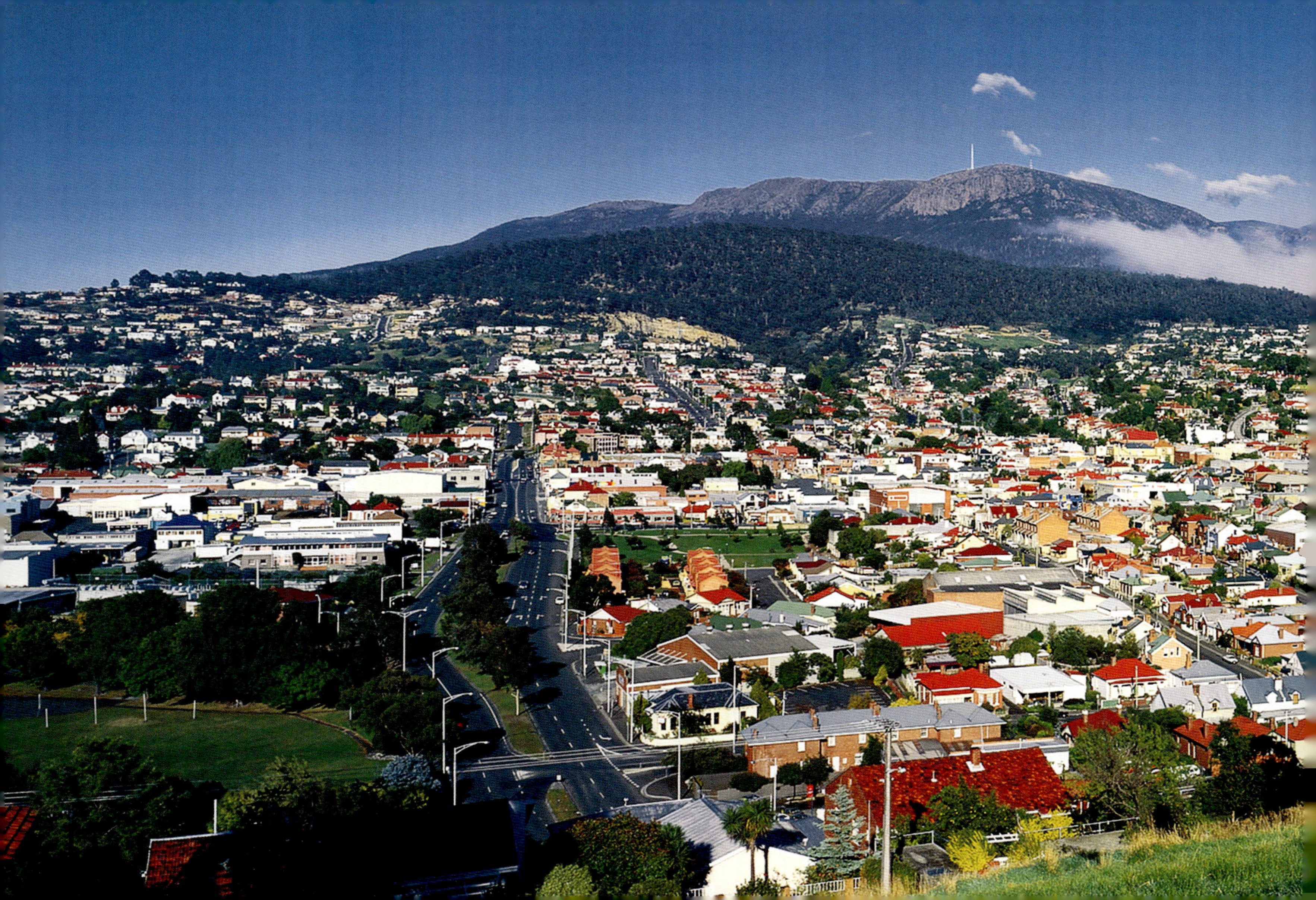

Hobart was built at the foothills of Mount Wellington.

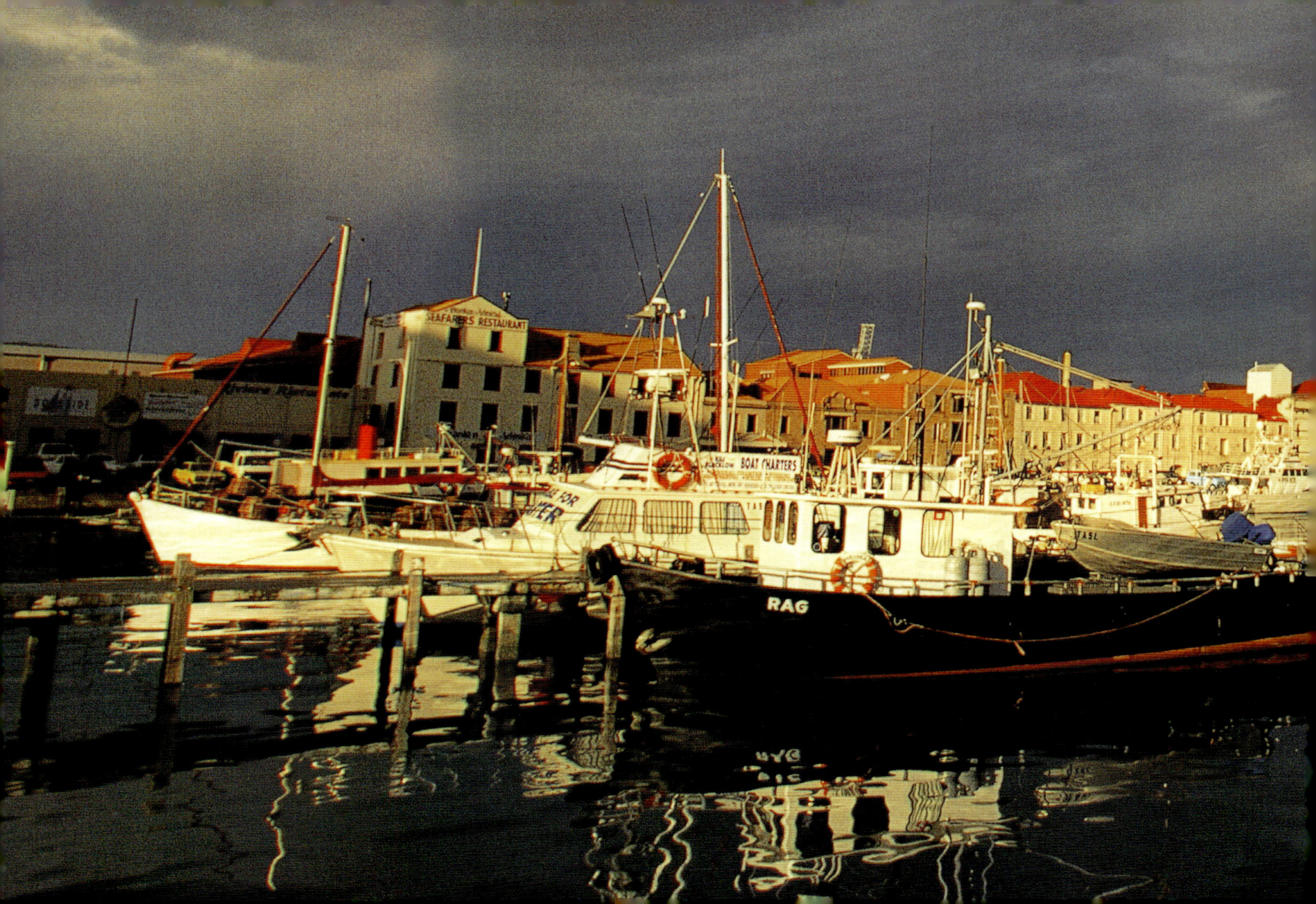
SEAFARERS RESTAURANT
BOAT CHARTERS
RAG

Sleepy Victoria Dock is home to Hobart's fishing fleet. However, during the annual Sydney-Hobart Yacht Race it becomes a hive of activity.

Once Australia's largest penal station, Port Arthur is now Tasmania's top tourist attraction.

Port Arthur was reserved for the hardest of criminals and was known for its harsh conditions.

Above: The ruins of the penal settlement at Port Arthur, which date from the 1800s, are now being painstakingly preserved. They are a powerful reminder of the country's convict past.

Right: The Devils Kitchen is just one of several dramatic rock formations on the Tasman Peninsula.

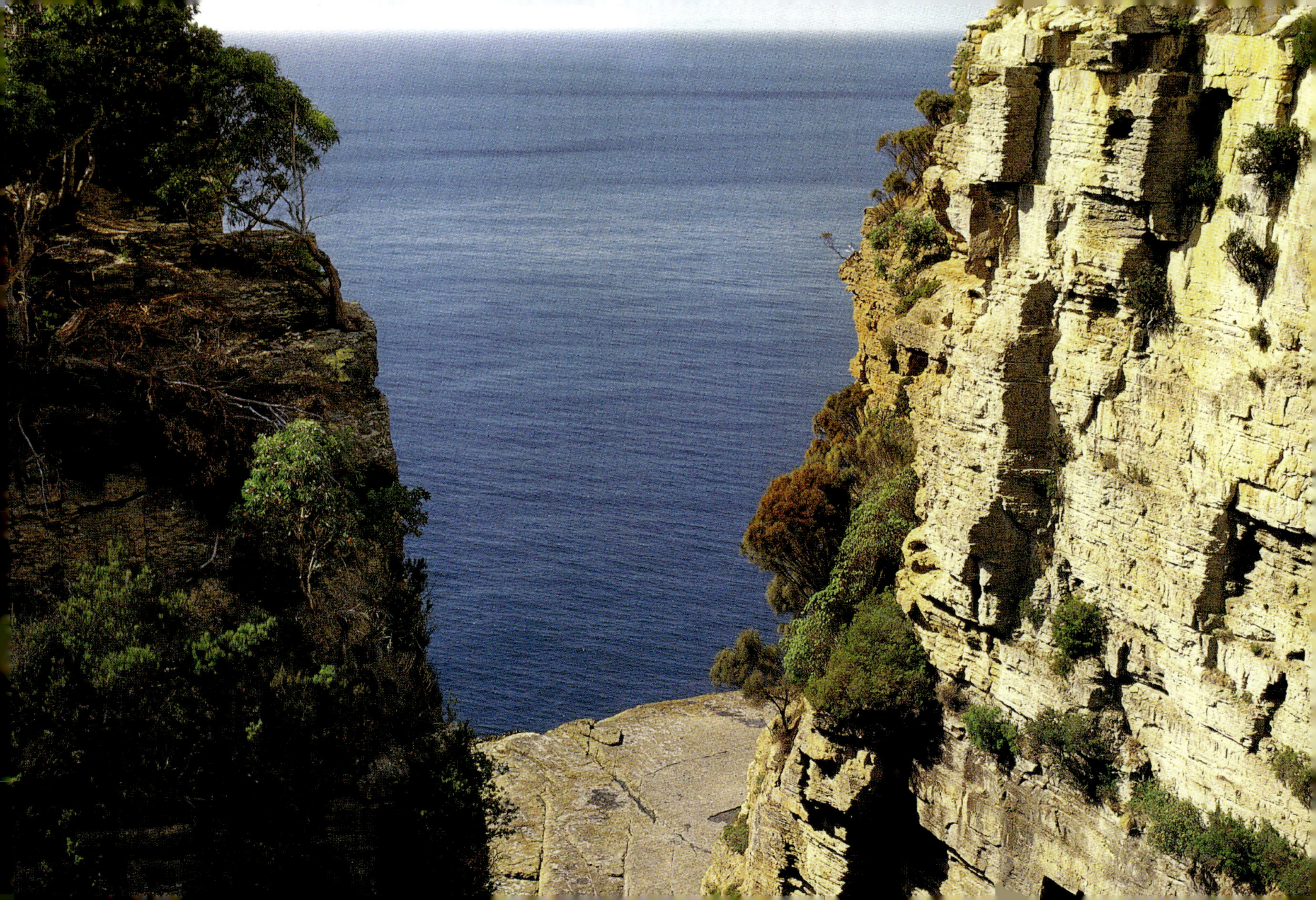

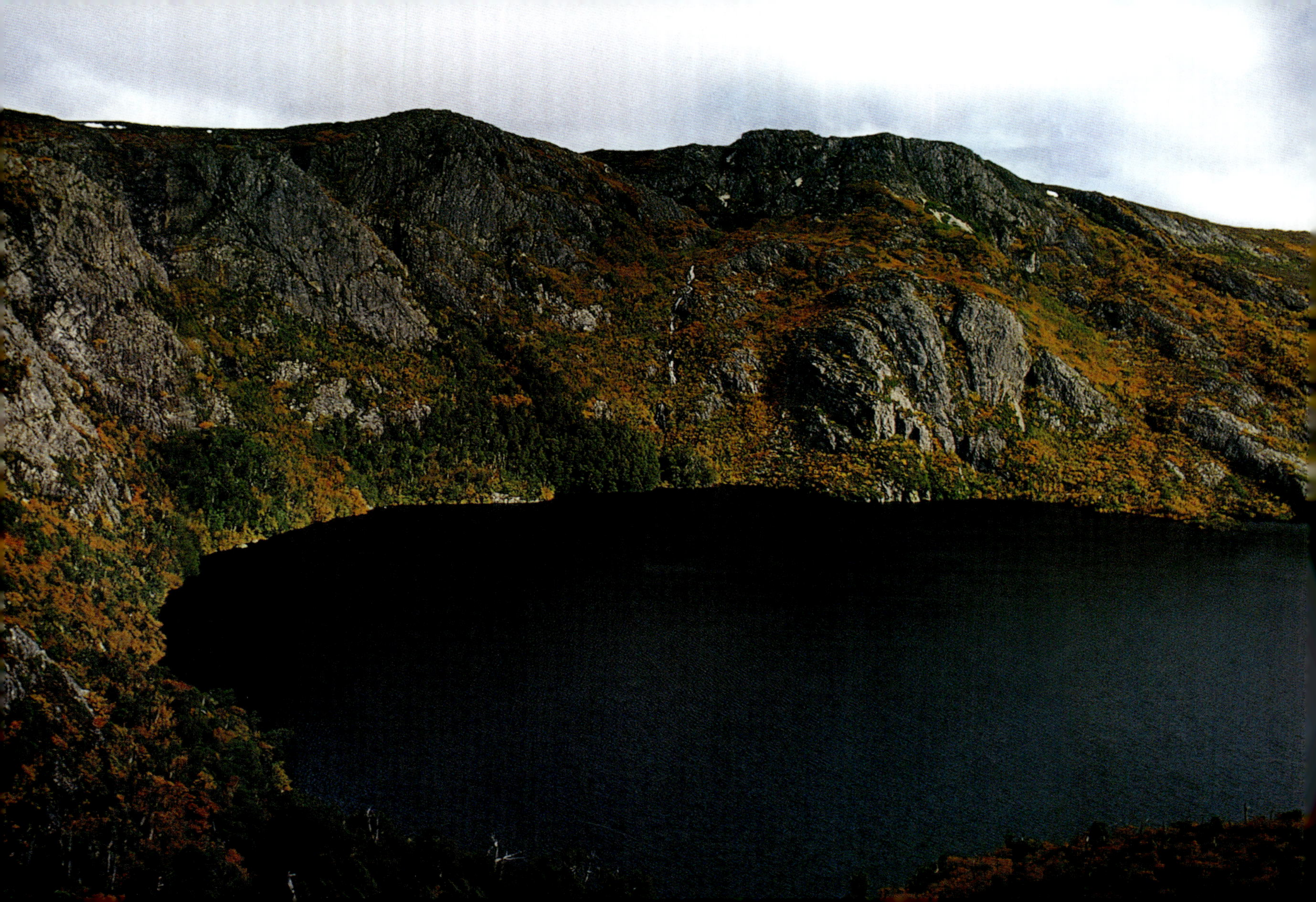

Right: Red-necked Wallabies are a common sight in the open woodland areas of Tasmania.

Left: Crater Lake in Cradle Mountain-Lake St Clair National Park is one of the highlights of the demanding 85-kilometre Overland Walking Track.

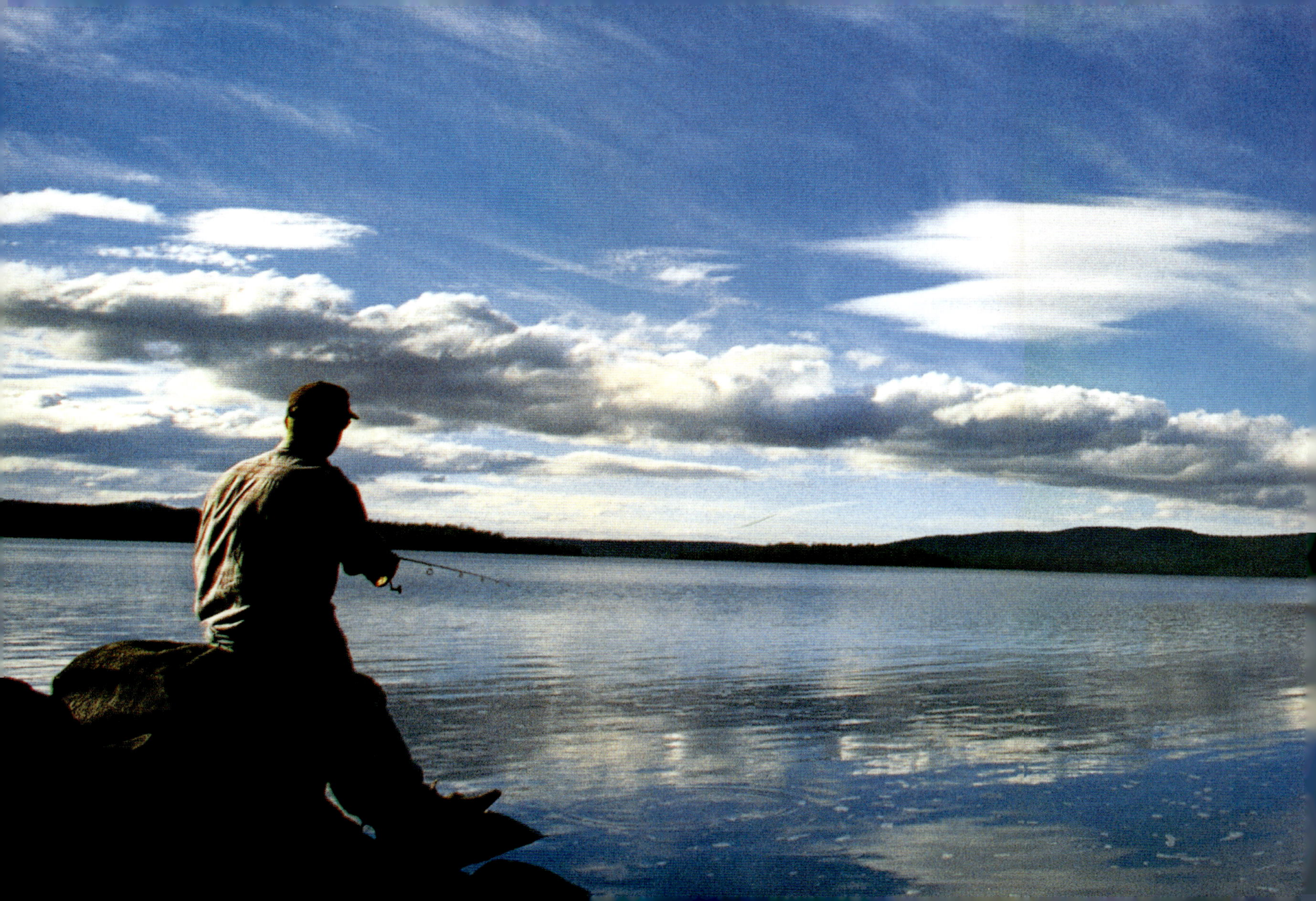

Tasmania, with its many unpolluted lakes, is widely believed to offer some of the best wild trout fishing in the world.

New Norfolk in the Derwent Valley is surrounded by rich farming land.

Mount Rowland, near Deloraine, lies in prime dairy farming country in the central north of Tasmania.

The Lady Stelfox paddlewheeler cruises down Cataract Gorge.

Gunpowder Mill is a magnet for visitors to Launceston.

The Tasman Coastal Trail, which finishes at Cape Pillar, takes three to five days to walk one way

Cradle Mountain is popular with hikers in summer and snowshoers in winter.

Lake Sorrell.

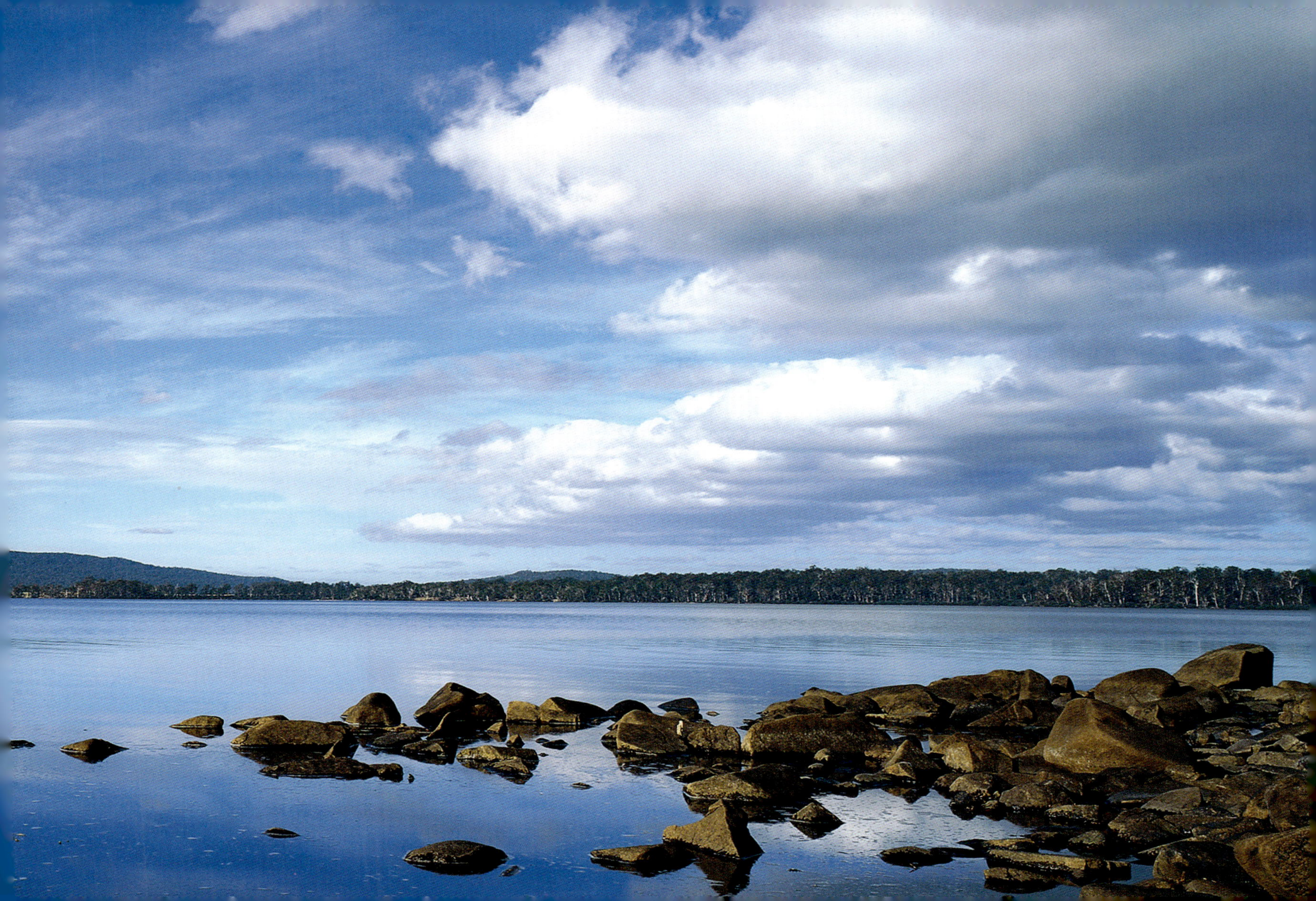

Adelaide.

Above left: The clearly visible spires of St Peter's Cathedral make it easy to understand why Adelaide is known as the 'City of Churches'.

Above right: The Adelaide Festival Centre is one of the venues for the city's biennial Arts Festival which attracts both local and international performers.

Above: The Barossa Valley was originally settled by German immigrants. The architecture of Chateau Yaldara displays this influence.

Right: Much of Australia's top wine is produced by the vineyards of the Barossa Valley.

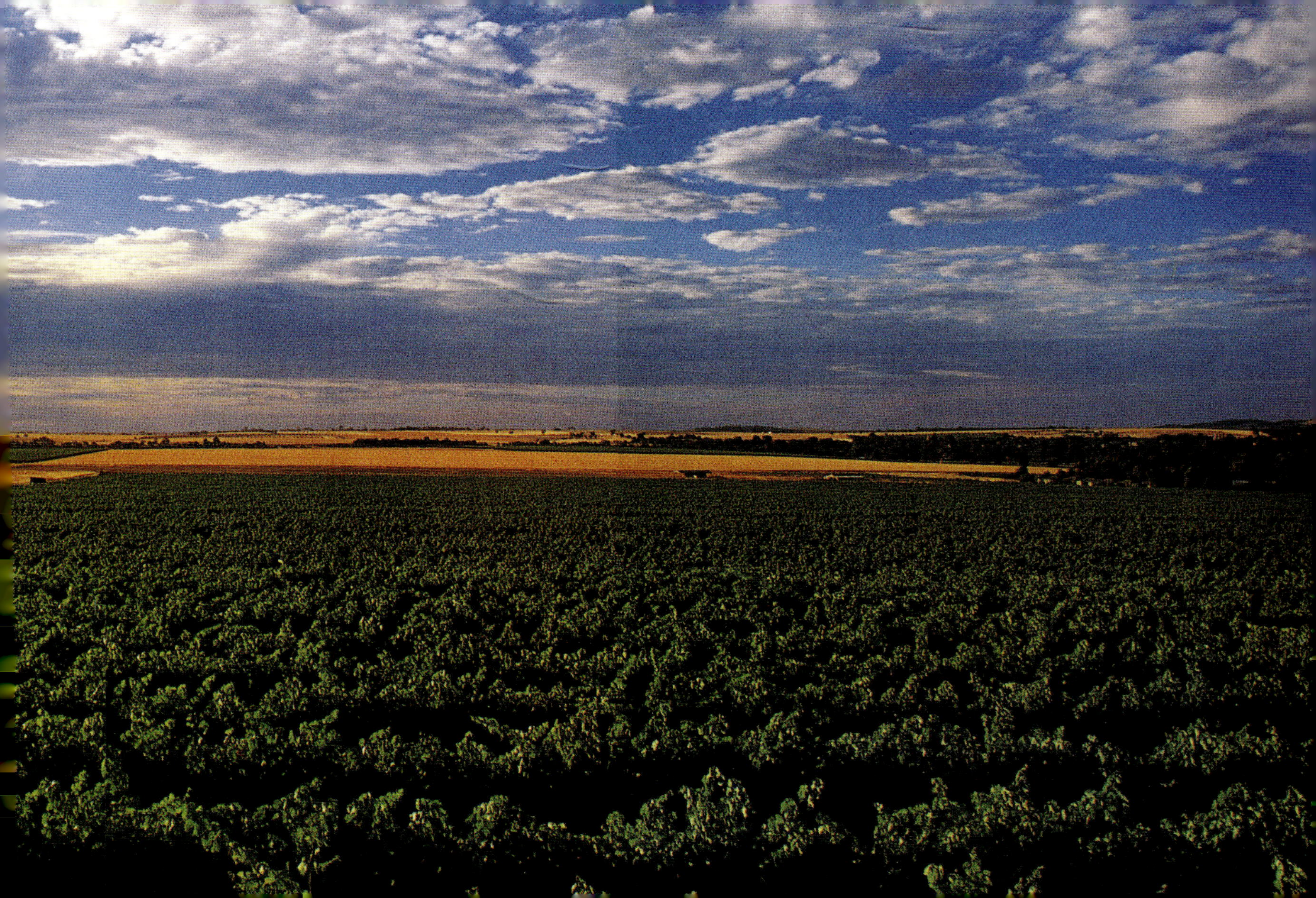

The treacherous coastline of Kangaroo Island has claimed many a ship.

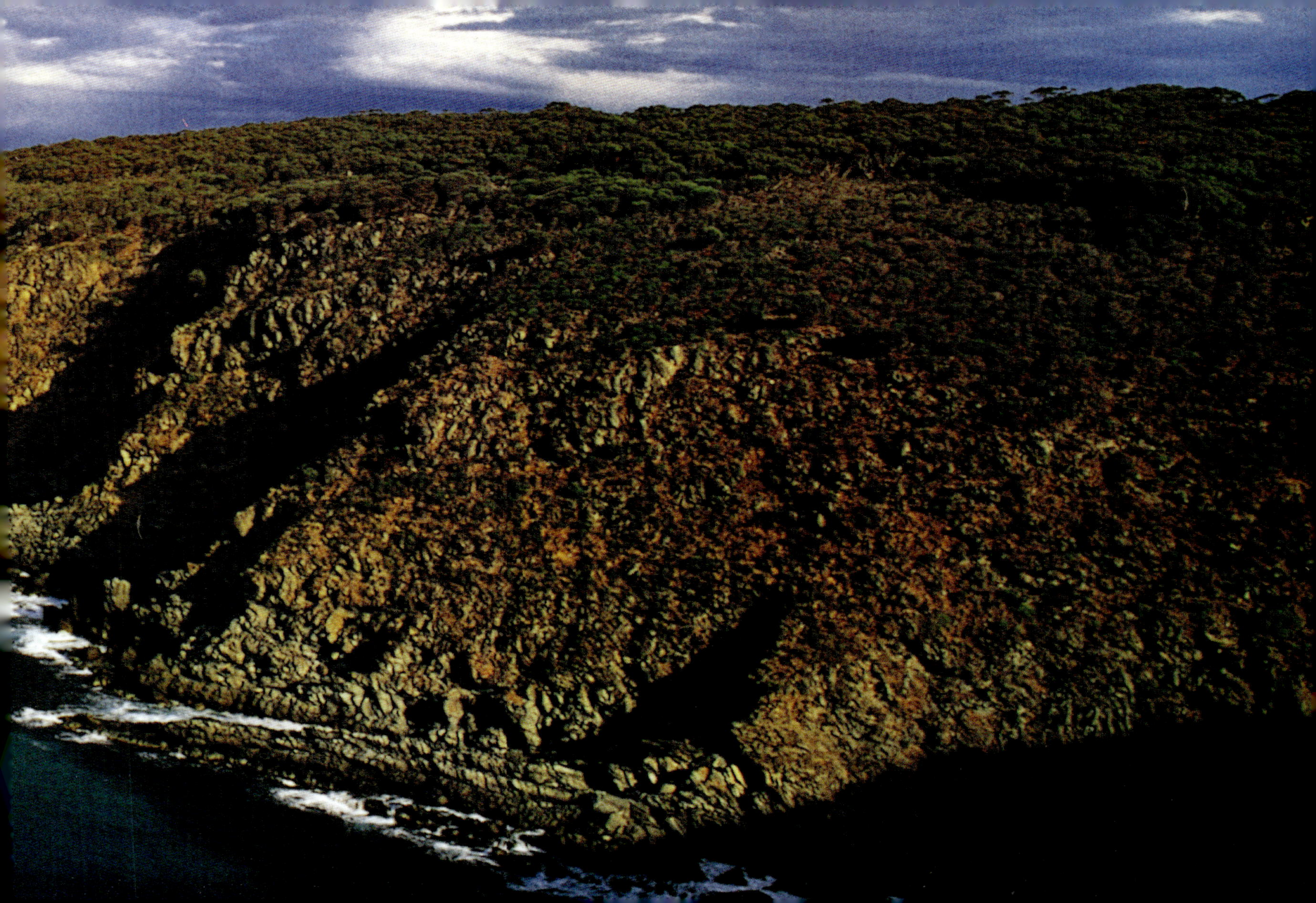

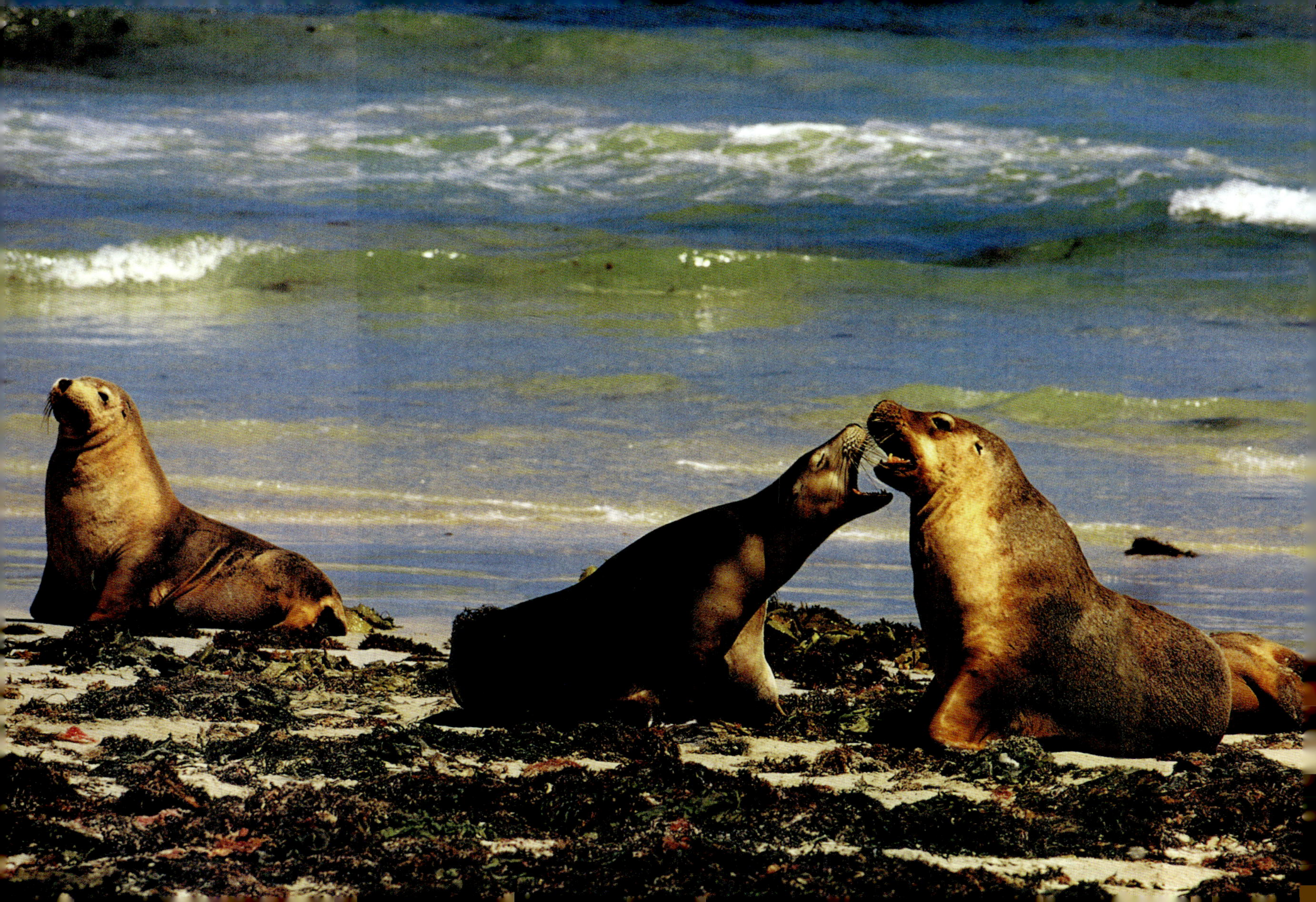

Right: Caves, sinkholes and limestone rock formations are a feature of the island—all created by the erosive power of the elements.

Left: Approximately 500 sea lions make their home at the island's Seal Bay. Accustomed to the presence of humans, these animals are protected by the conservation park.

SKYCITY is South Australia's only casino and is in an historic railway station.

The Mount Lofty summit is on the highest peak in the Adelaide Hills.

Perth's Bell Tower.

Burswood International Resort Casino.

Western Australian Maritime Museum.

Perth at night

The Swan River was named after the black swans so common to Western Australia.

The glorious colours of Calytrix wildflowers.

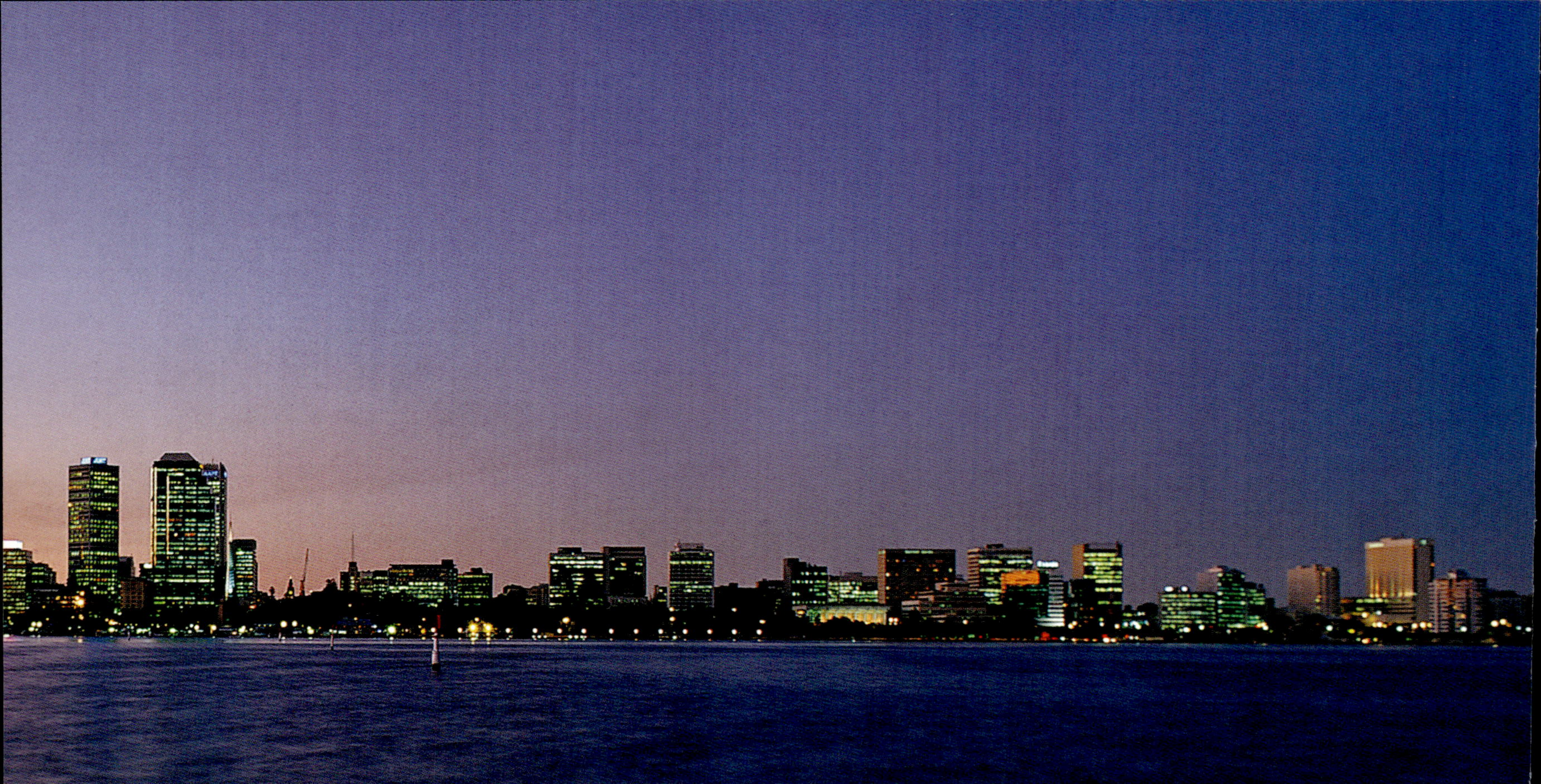

Above: Built by convicts as a gaol, Fremantle's Round House is now the state's oldest surviving building.

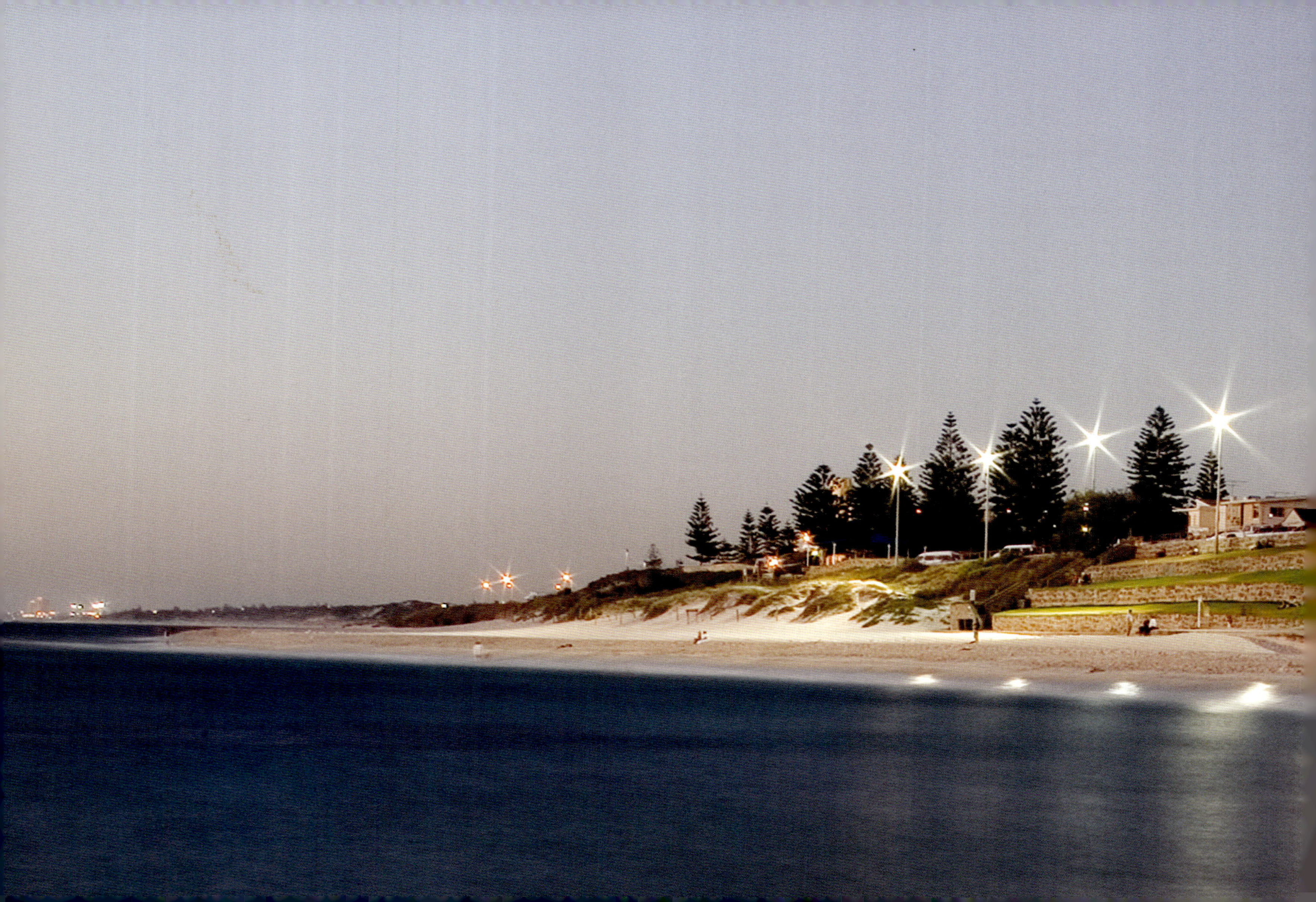

Fremantle at dusk.

Gantheaume Bay Beach near Broome in north-western Australia.

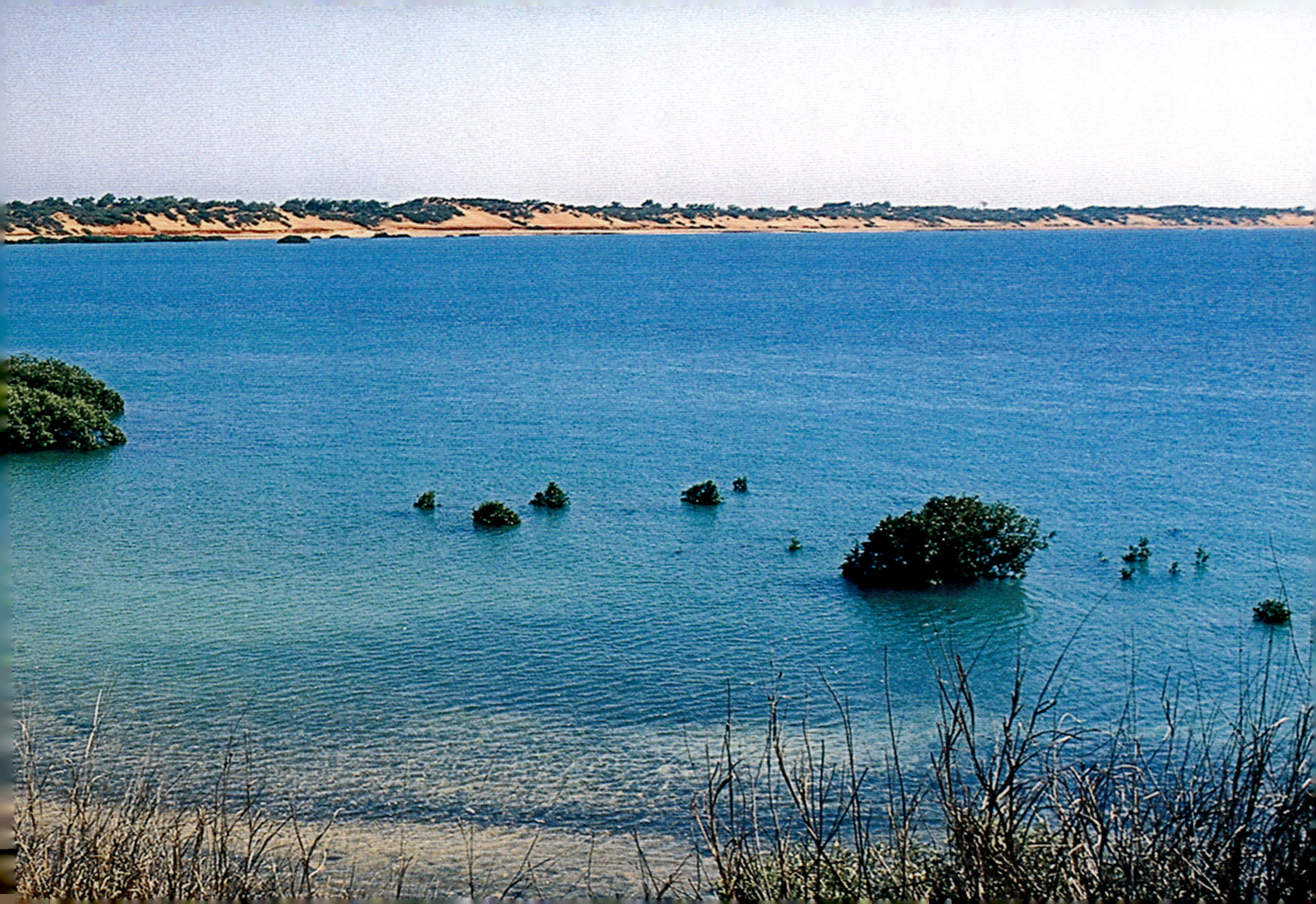

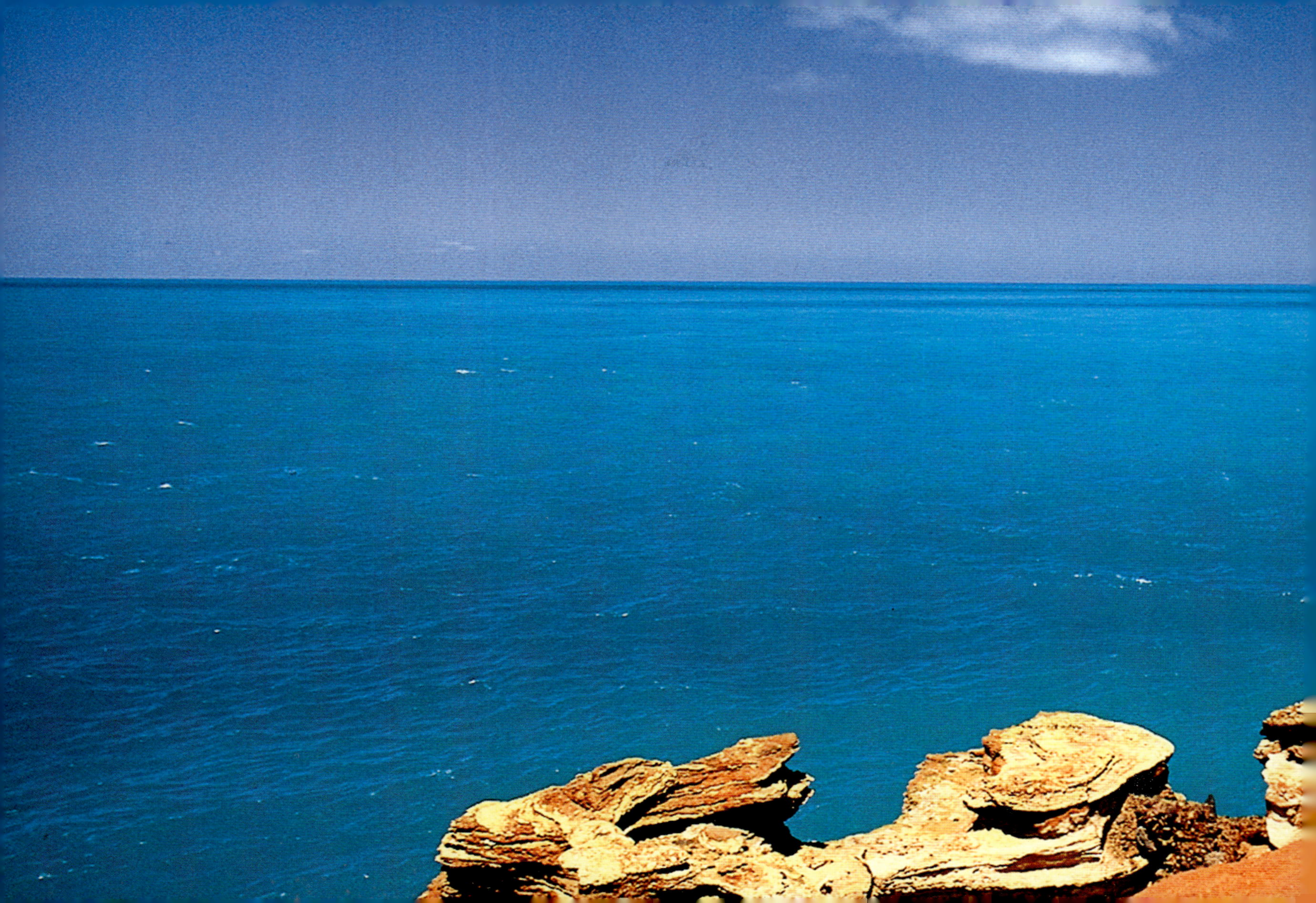

The red earth commonly seen in Western Australia provides a dramatic contrast with the blue ocean.

Above: Rottnest Island is home to large colonies of quokkas, a small species of marsupial.

Top and right: Only 19 kilometres from Perth, tranquil Rottnest Island with its unspoilt bays and crystal-clear water is a popular weekend getaway.

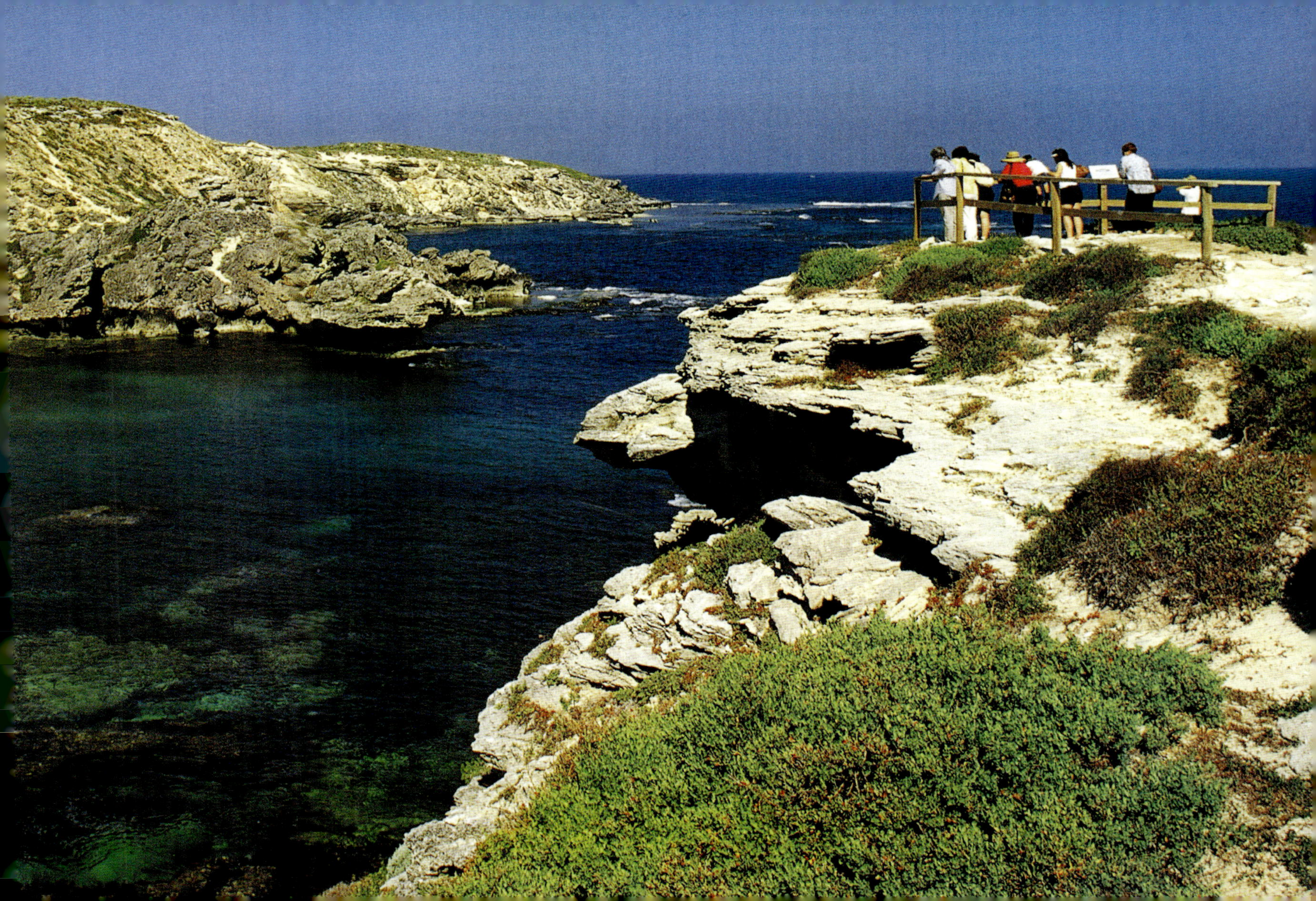

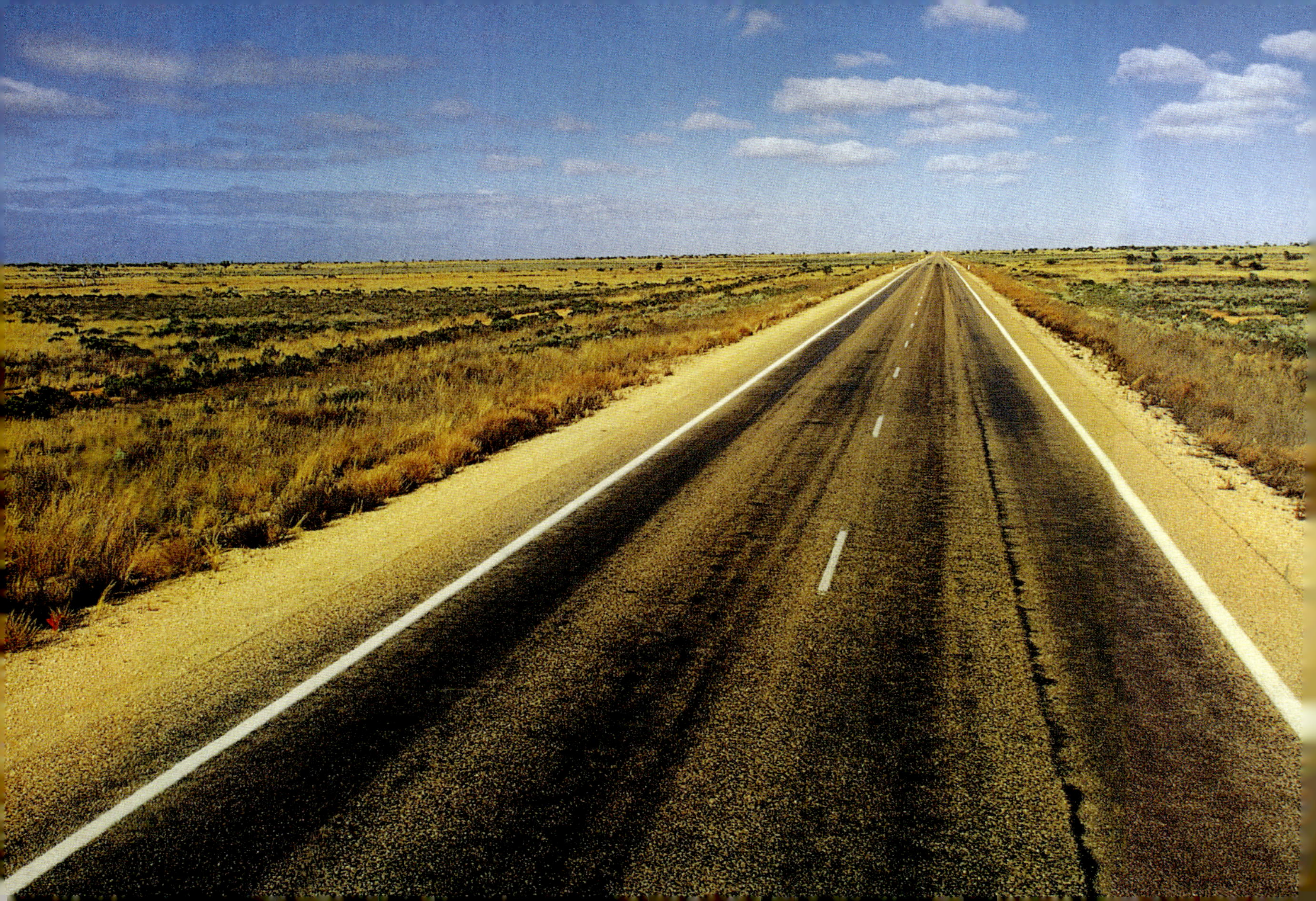

Top right: Driving across the Nullarbor, the unwary motorist can encounter several unusual hazards!

Right: Wave Rock near Hyden is a granite 'breaker' that has been sculpted by wind erosion.

Left: The road stretches in an unwavering line for miles across the featureless Nullarbor Plain.

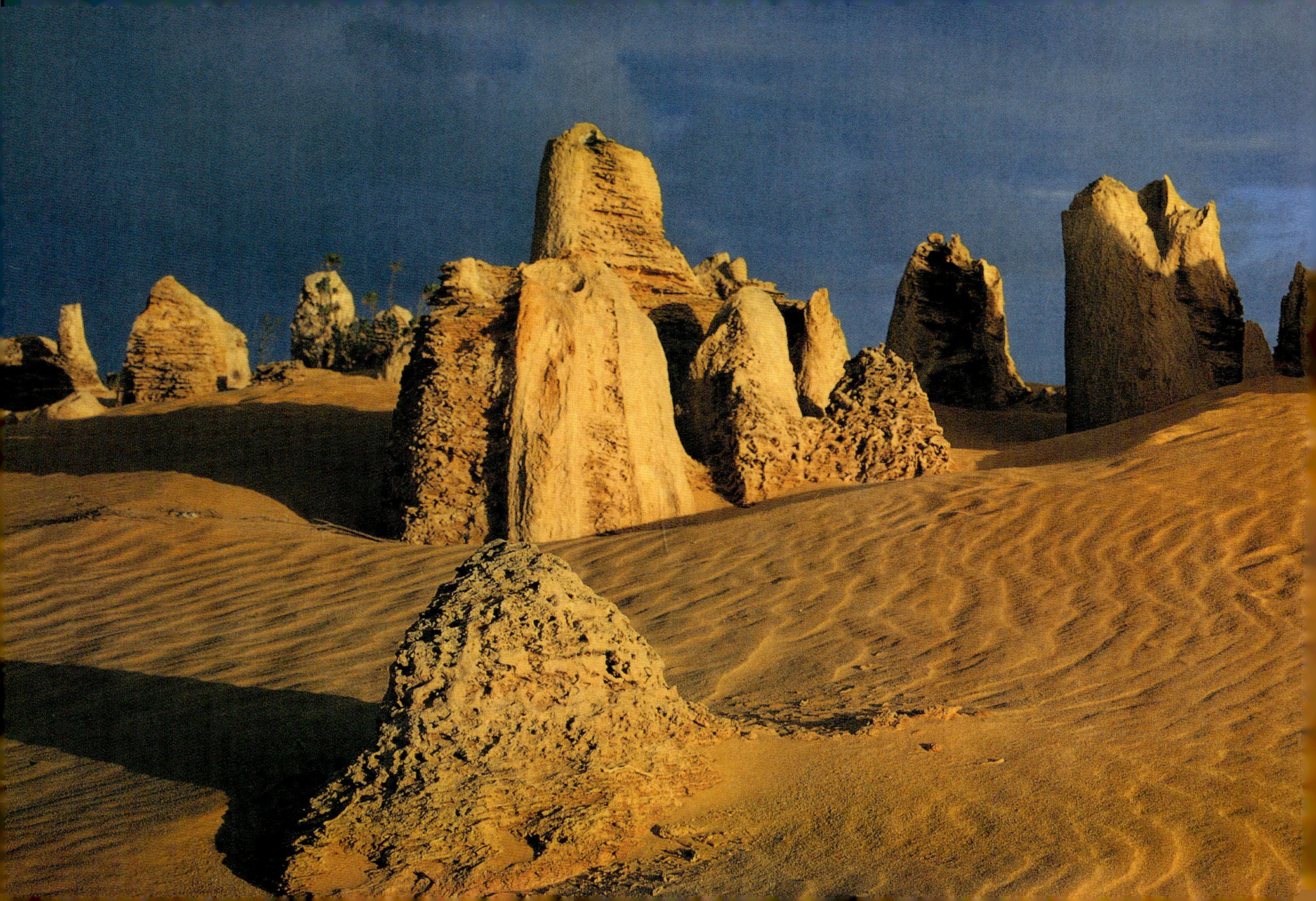

Limestone pillars known as the Pinnacles rise out of the desert in Nambung National Park, casting eerie shadows across the sand.

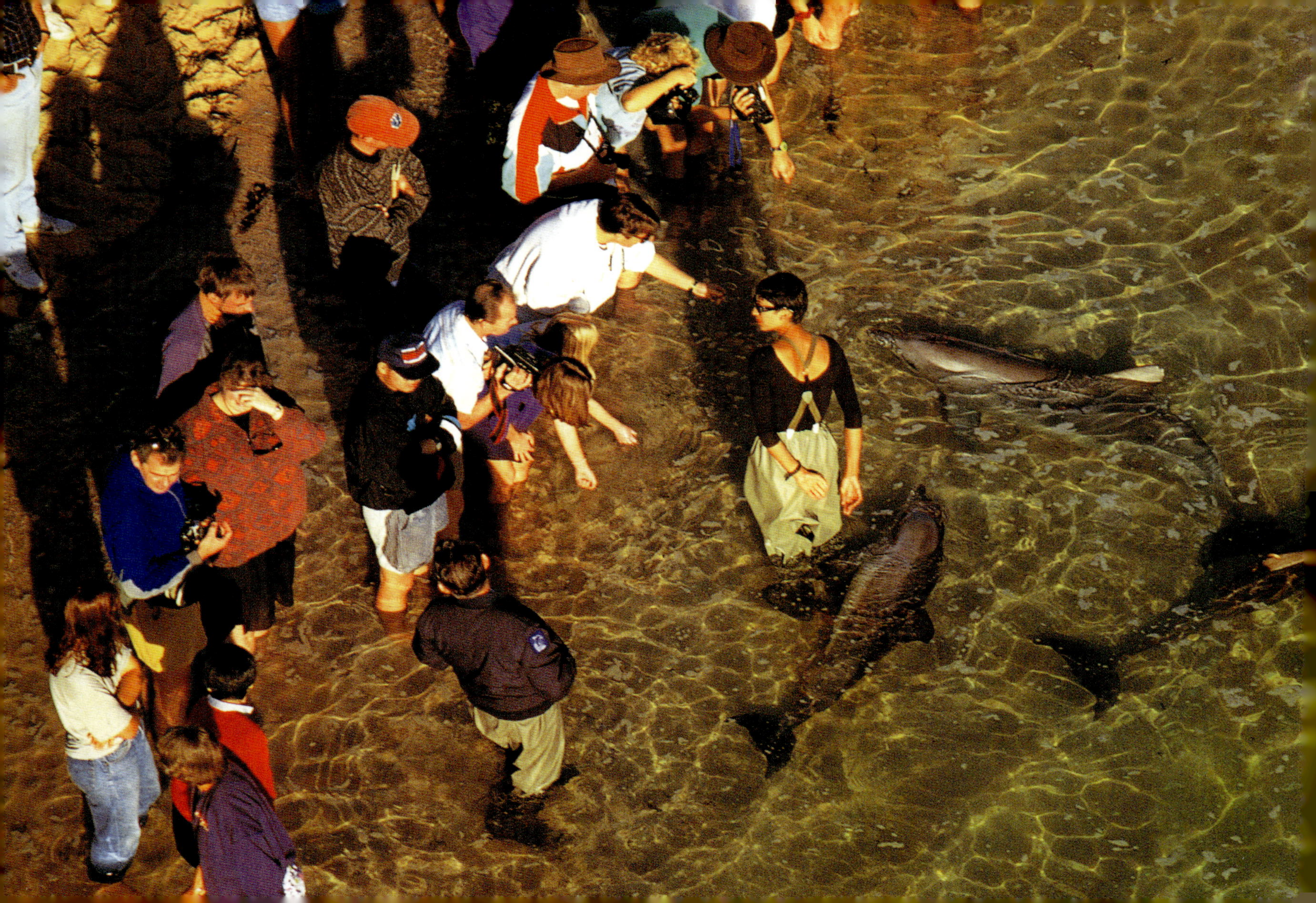

Above: The stromatolites of Hamelin Pool date back some 3,500 million years, making them the world's second-oldest known fossil. Hamelin Pool forms part of the Shark Bay Marine Park.

Left: At Monkey Mia in Shark Bay, a thriving tourism industry has developed around the dolphins that swim to shore each day to be hand fed.

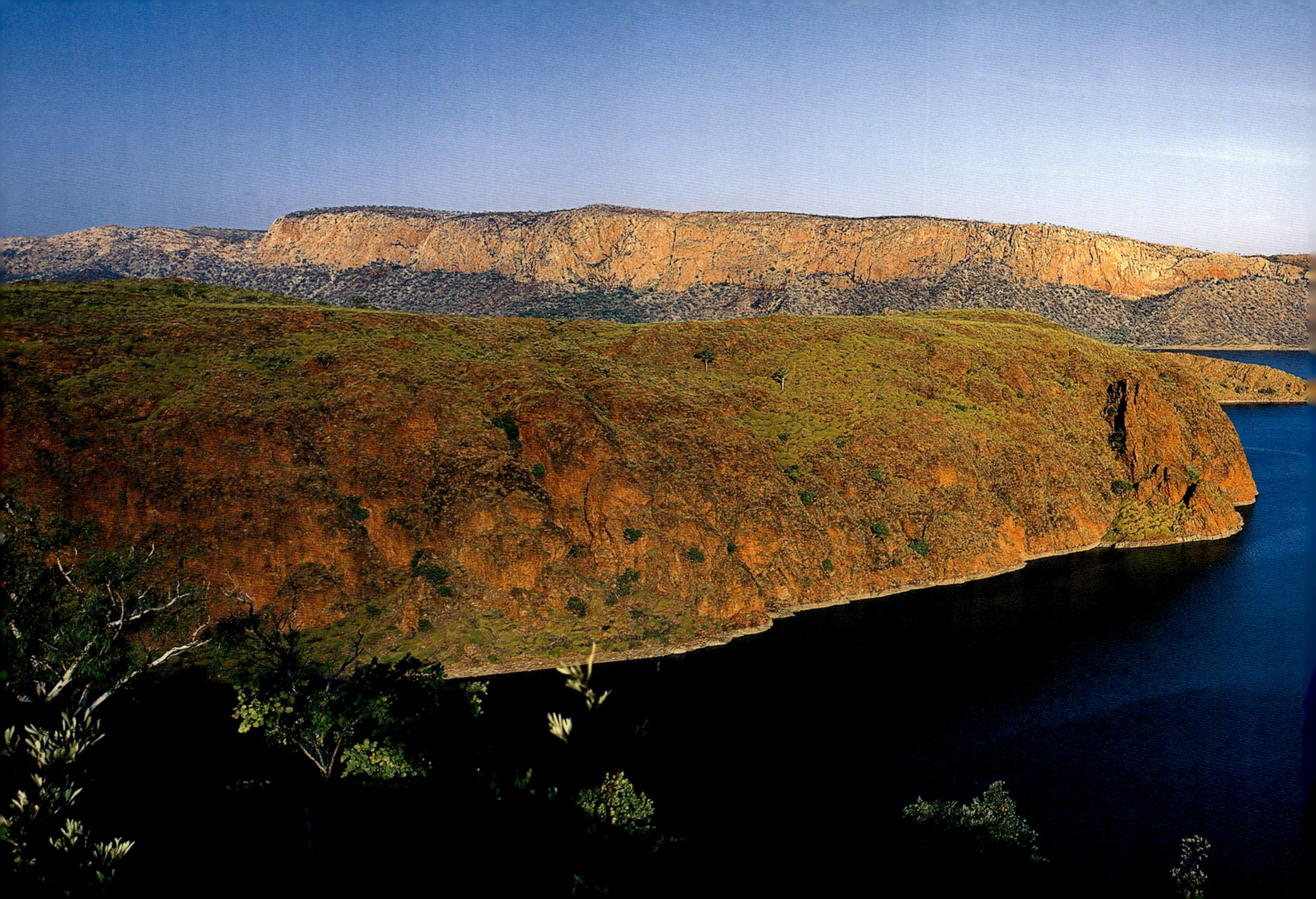

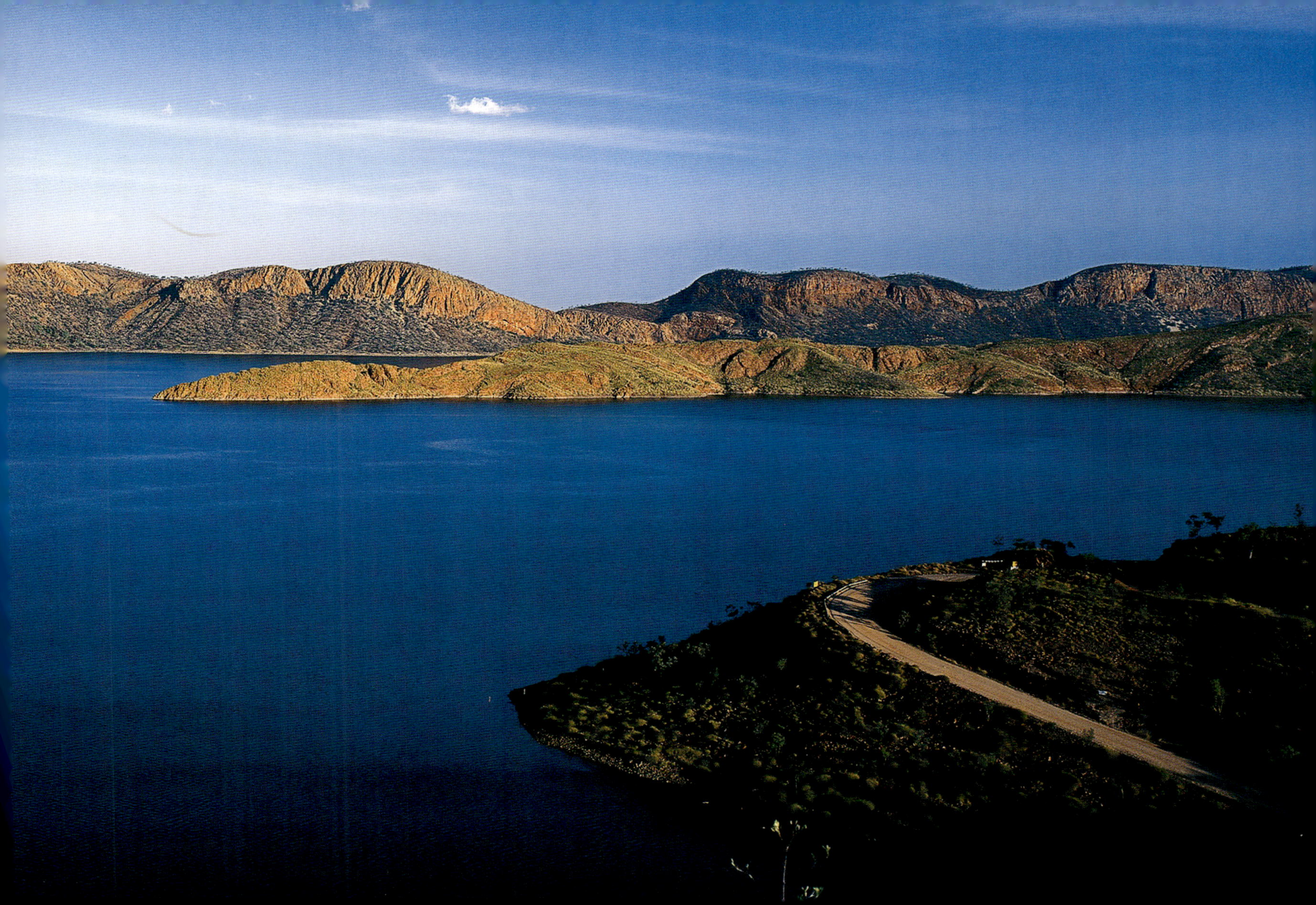

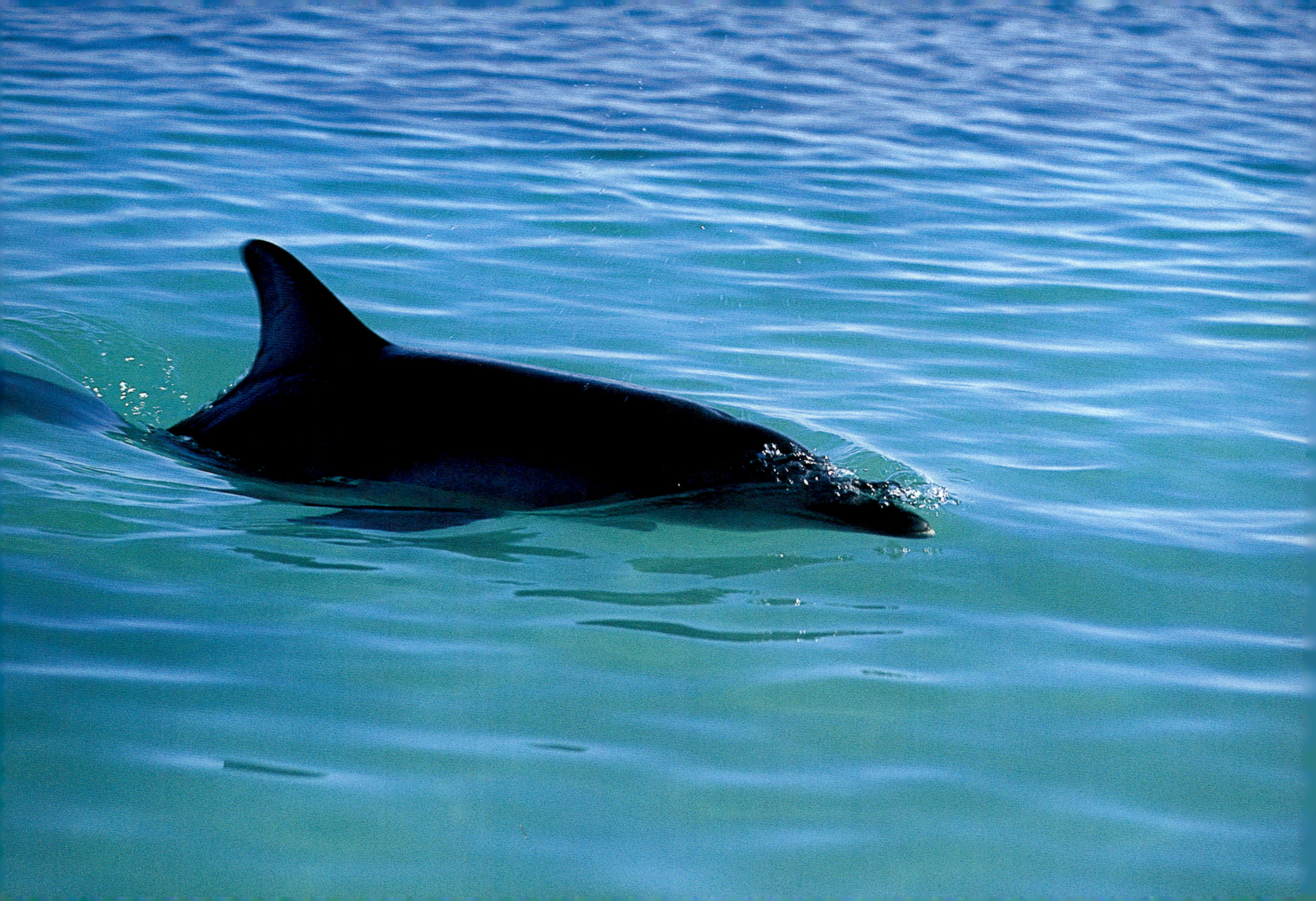

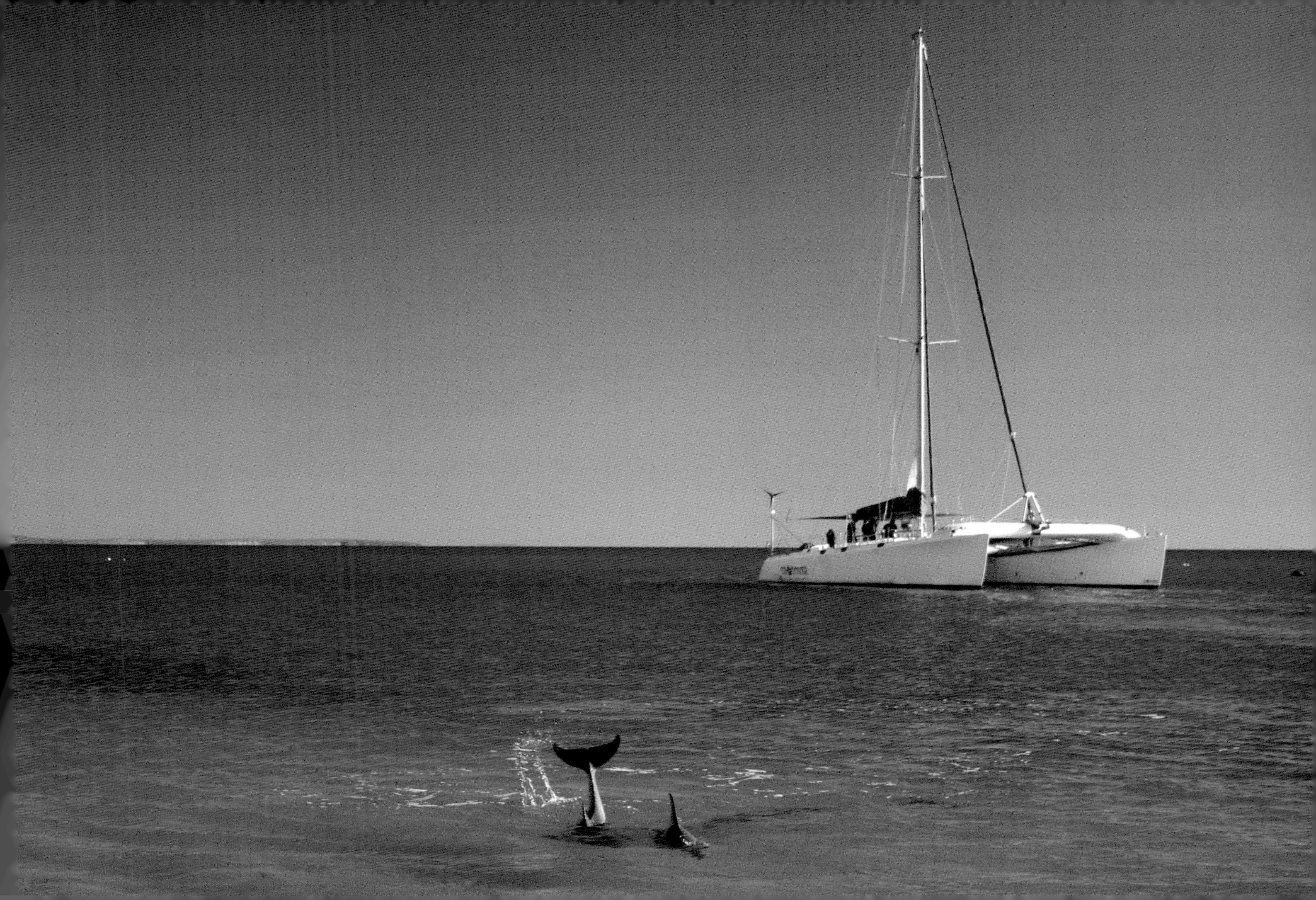

Above: Just outside Port Hedland, vast expanses of glistening salt wait to be shipped overseas.

Right: Once the pearling capital of the world, tourism is now increasingly important to Broome, with camel rides being offered along Cable Beach.

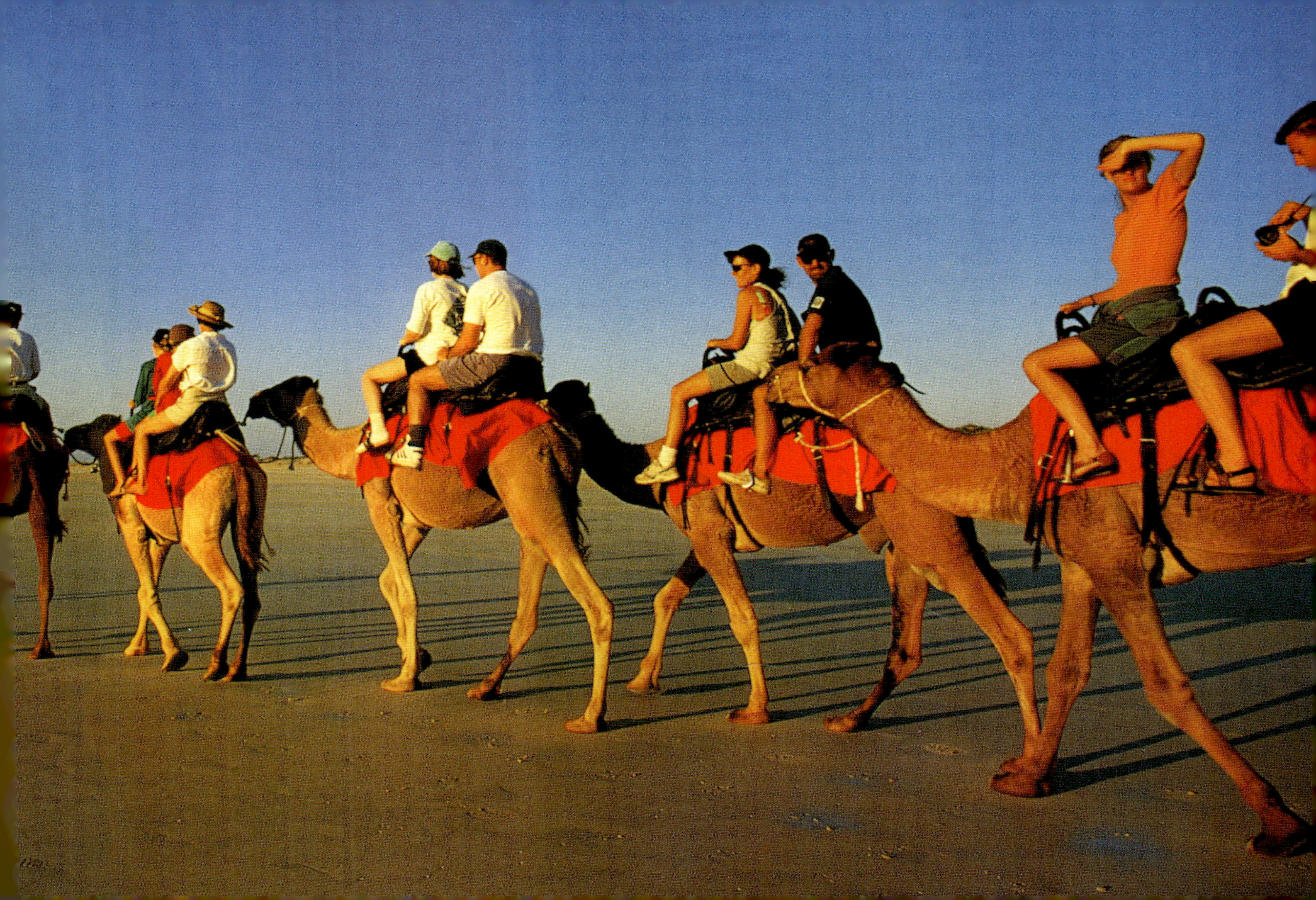

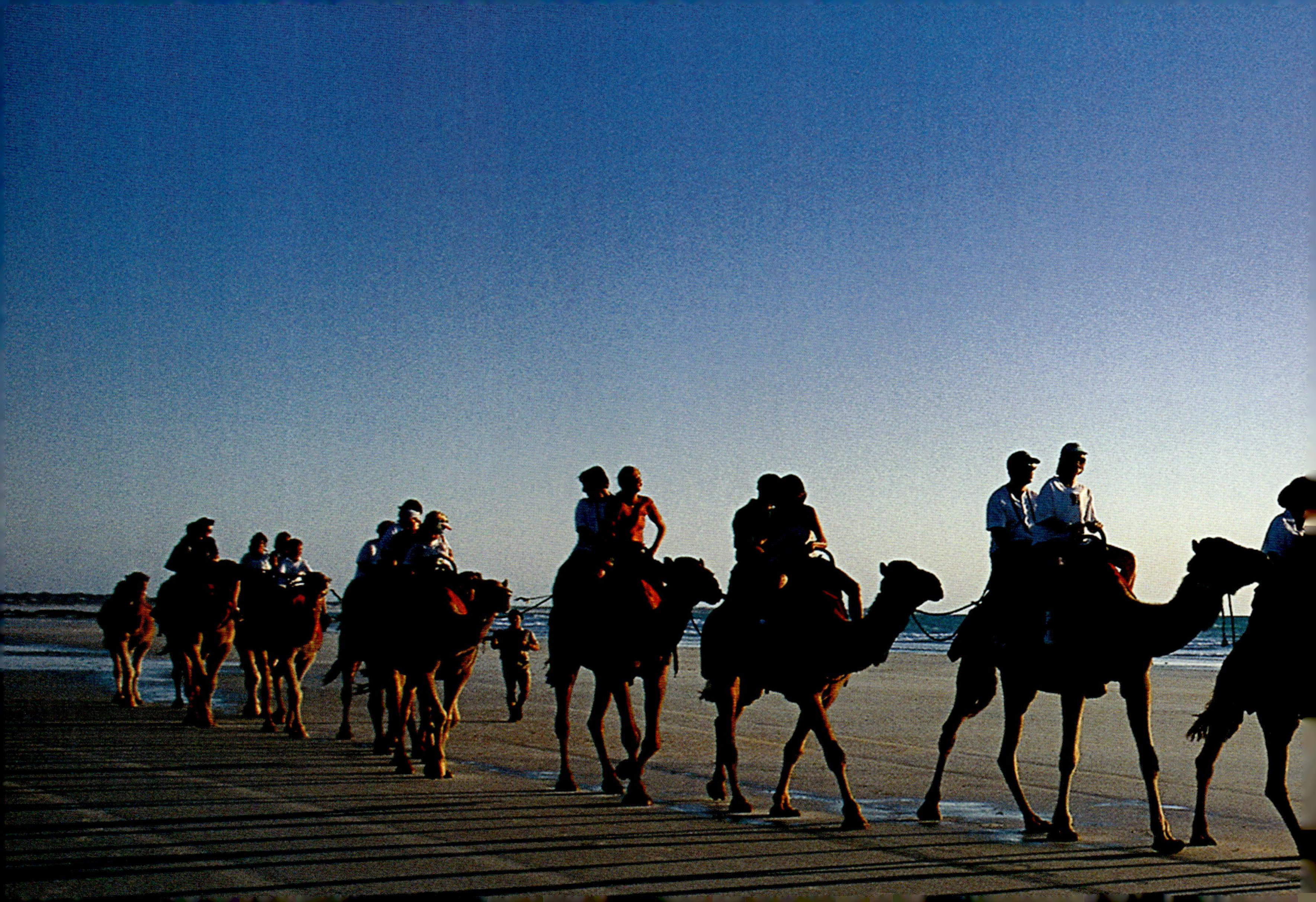

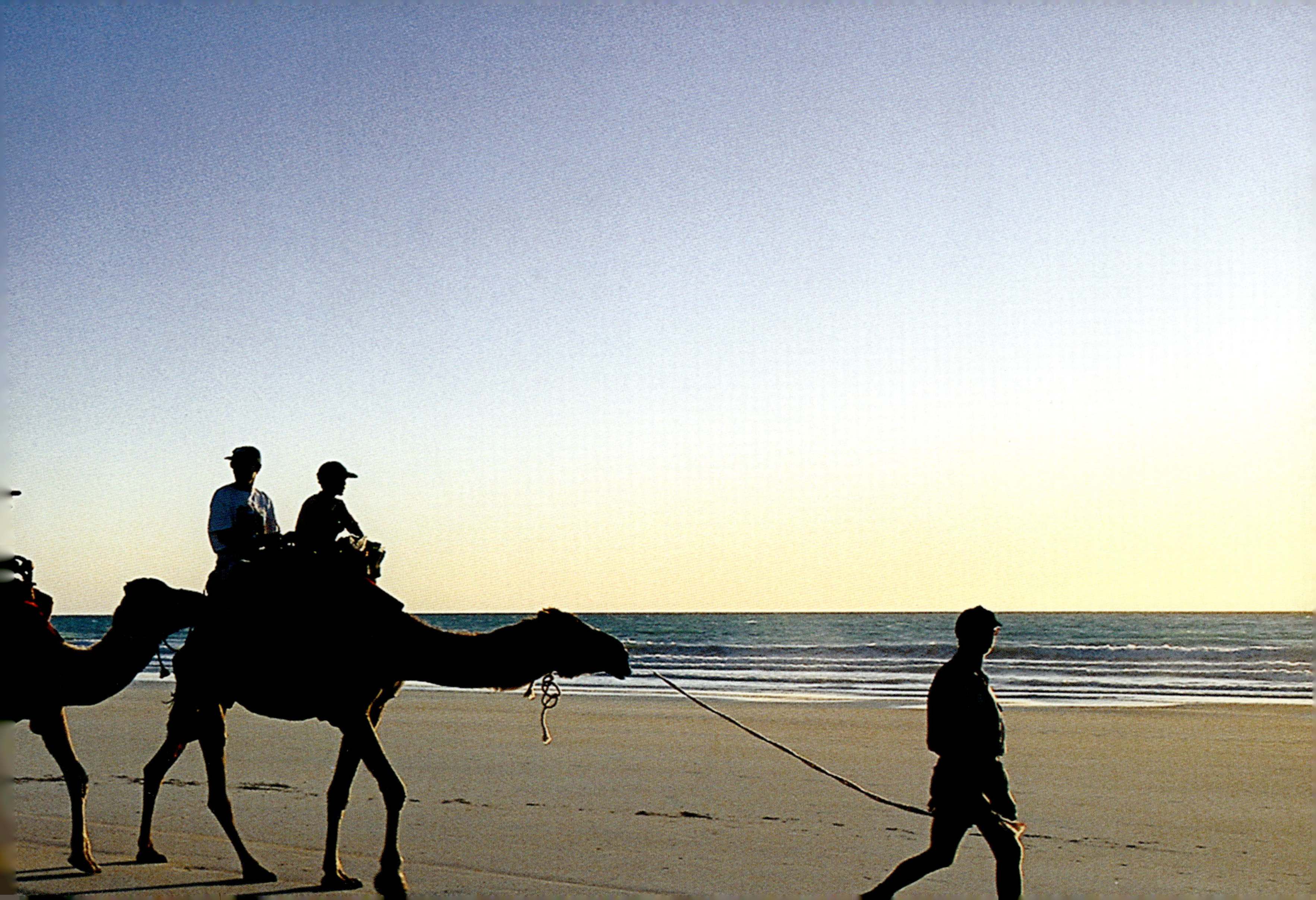

Fortescue Falls in Karijini National Park.

Above: The life of a 'jackeroo' on the vast Northern Territory cattle stations has changed little over the years.

Above left, and right: Nourlangie Rock in Kakadu National Park is an important Aboriginal rock-art site. Here, the 'Lightning Man' holds his arc of light.

Above right: From the lookout at Ubirr, the visitor can obtain sweeping views of Kakadu's wetlands which abound with animal and plantlife as soon as the first rains arrive.

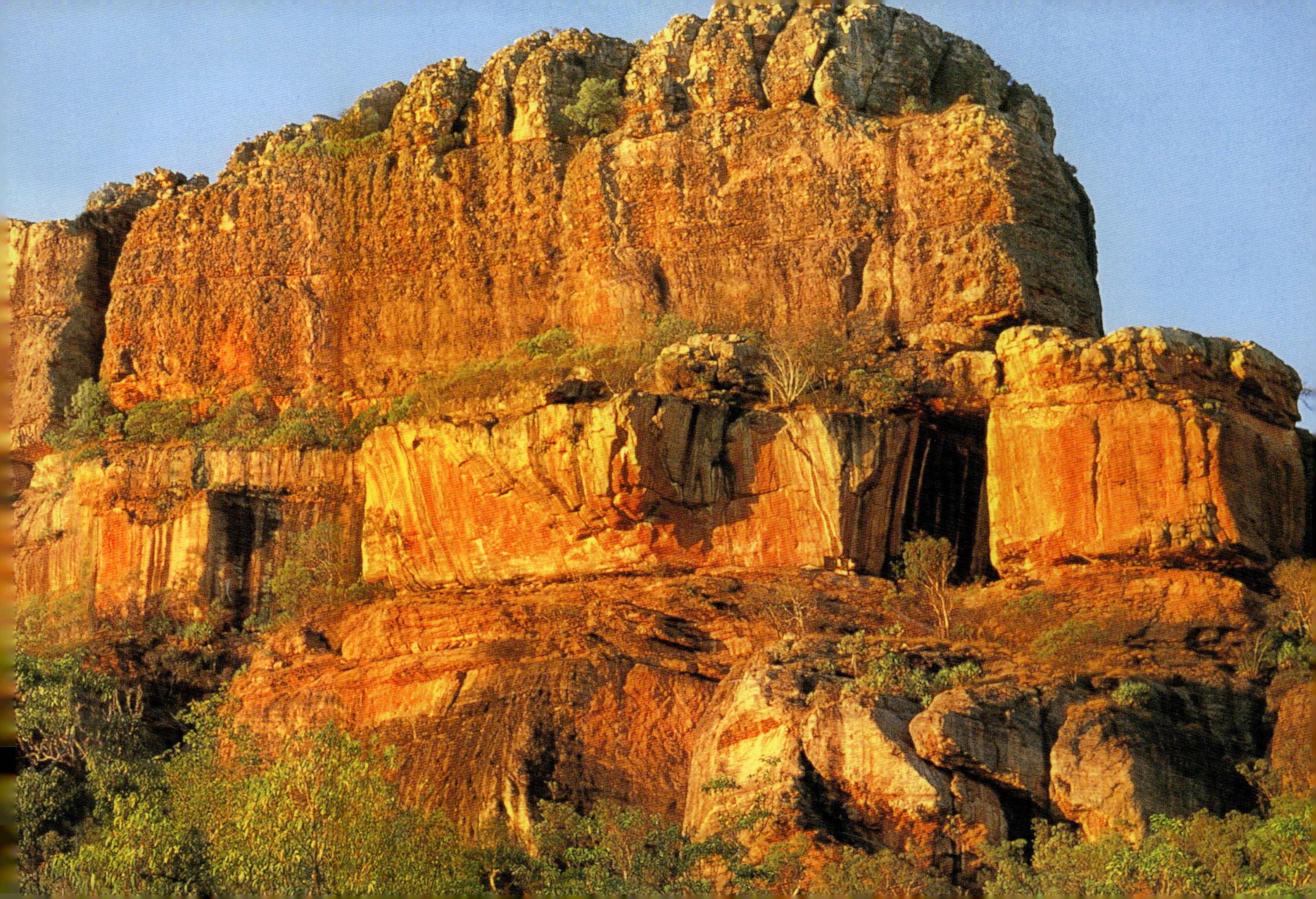

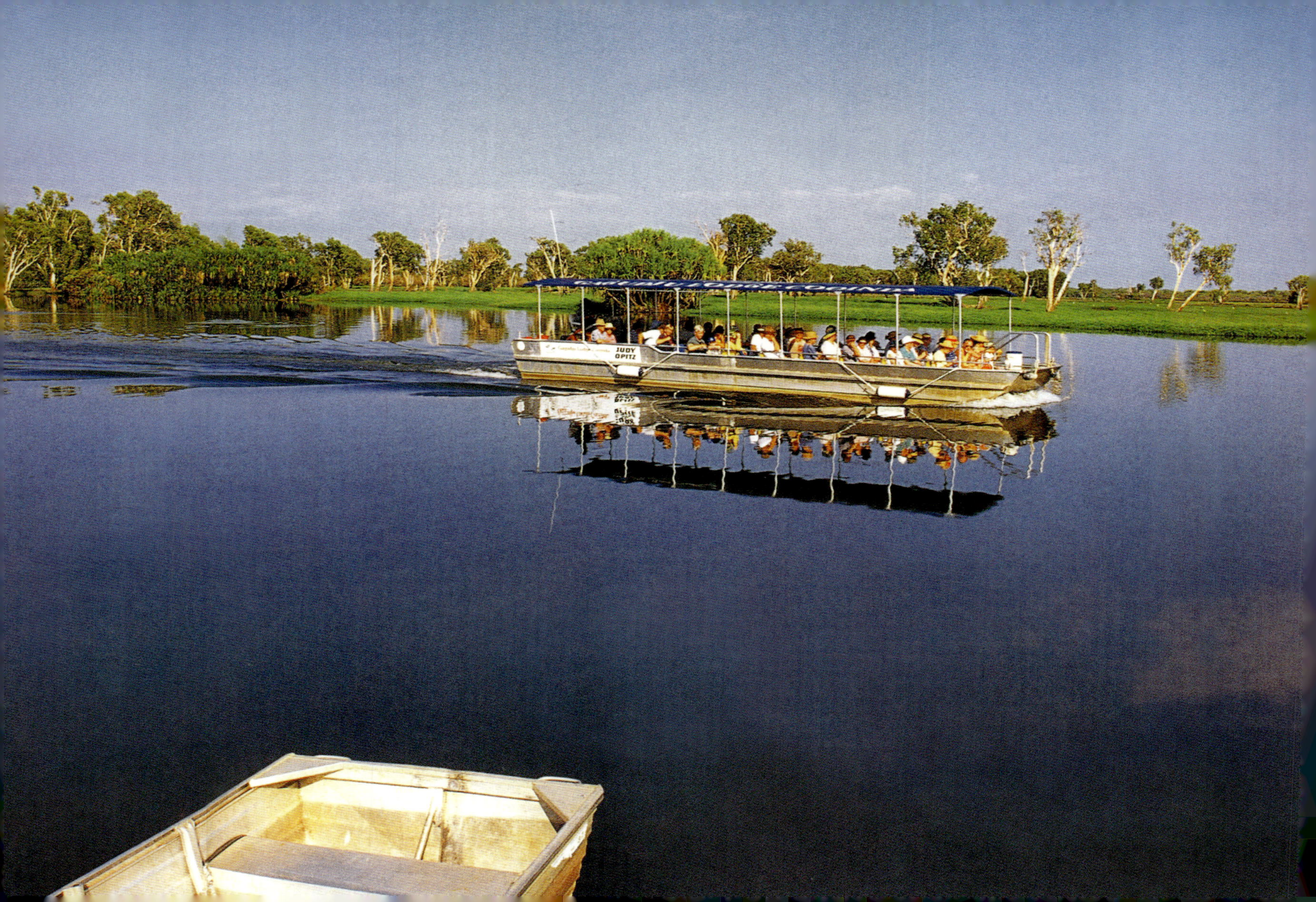
JUDY
OPITZ

Right: During the wet season, huge numbers of migratory waterbirds—including the black-necked stork, or jabiru—flock to Kakadu.

Left: A cruise on Yellow Waters enables visitors to observe the region's birdlife as well as its fearsome saltwater crocodiles.

Left and right: The rocky outcrops known as the Devils Marbles, near Tennant Creek, are—according to Aboriginal legend—the eggs of the Rainbow Serpent.

Top: South of Darwin lies Katherine Gorge which, over the millennia, has been carved out of the sandstone rock by the Katherine River.

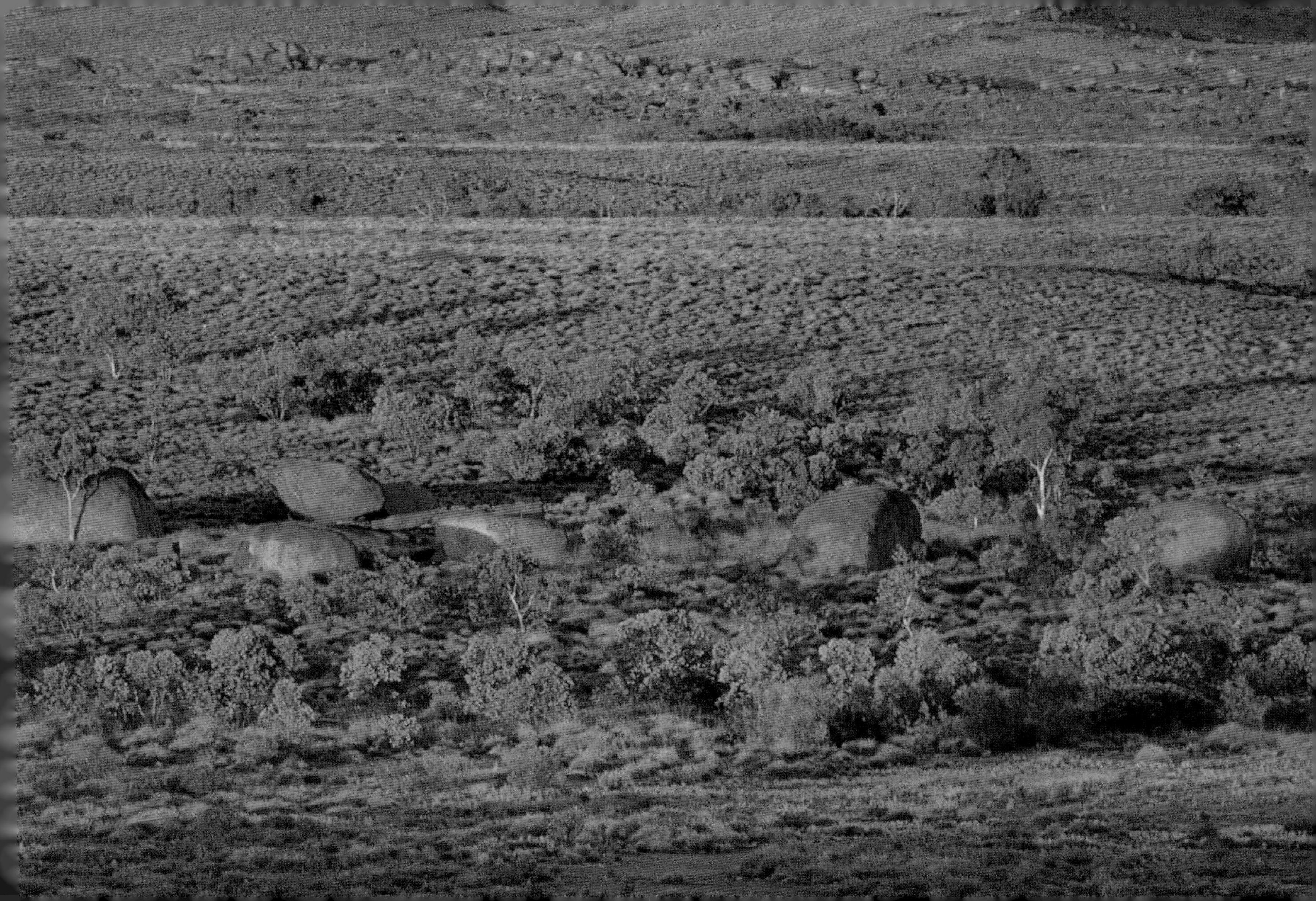

Darwin city centre.

Above: The majestic cliffs of Rainbow Valley are streaked with bands of colour, making them particularly impressive at sunrise and sunset.

The world's largest monolith, Uluru (formerly known as Ayers Rock) rises an imposing 348 metres above the surrounding landscape.

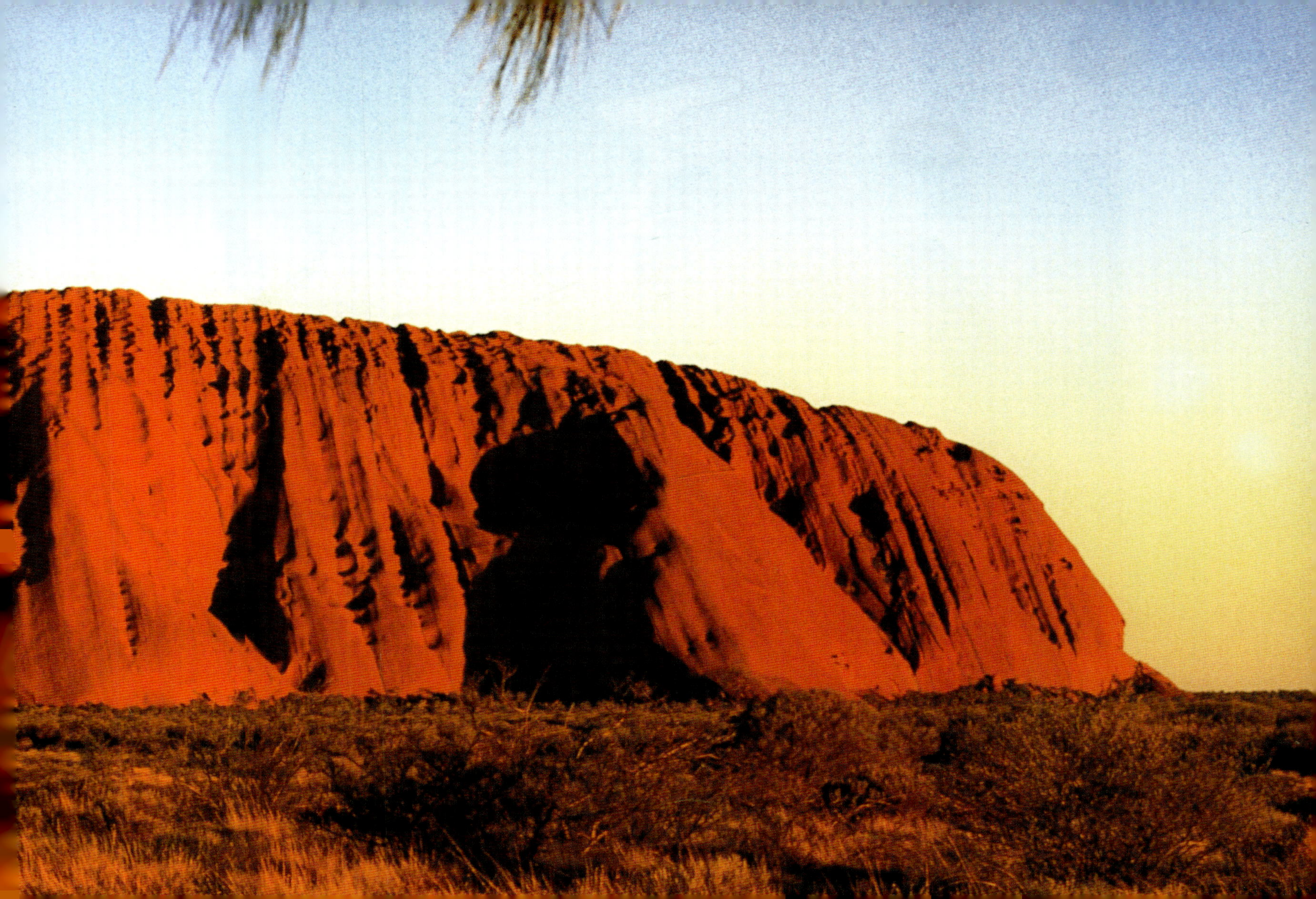

Left and right: Kata Tjuta means 'many heads' in the local Aboriginal language—an accurate description of this famous formation's numerous domes.

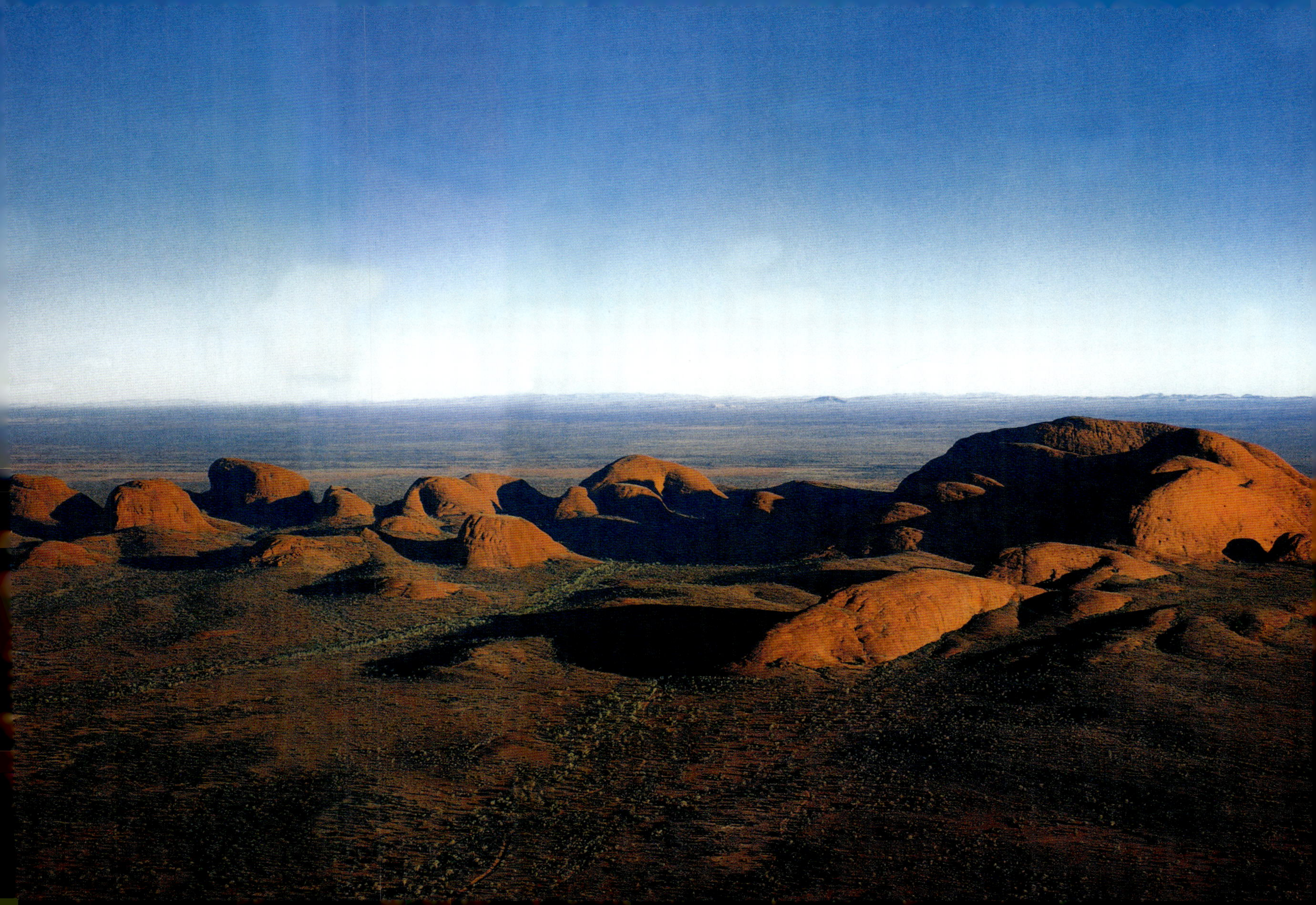

Kakadu National Park is remarkable for its biological and ecological diversity.

Twin Falls is accessible by four-wheel drive through Kakadu National Park.

Crocodiles make tourists think twice before swimming in the waters of the Northern Territory.

The Devil's Marbles south of Tennant Creek are made of granite thought to be formed 1.7 billion years ago.

The Story Bridge in Brisbane.

Brisbane city as seen at daylight hours.

Surfer's Paradise on Queensland's Gold Coast.

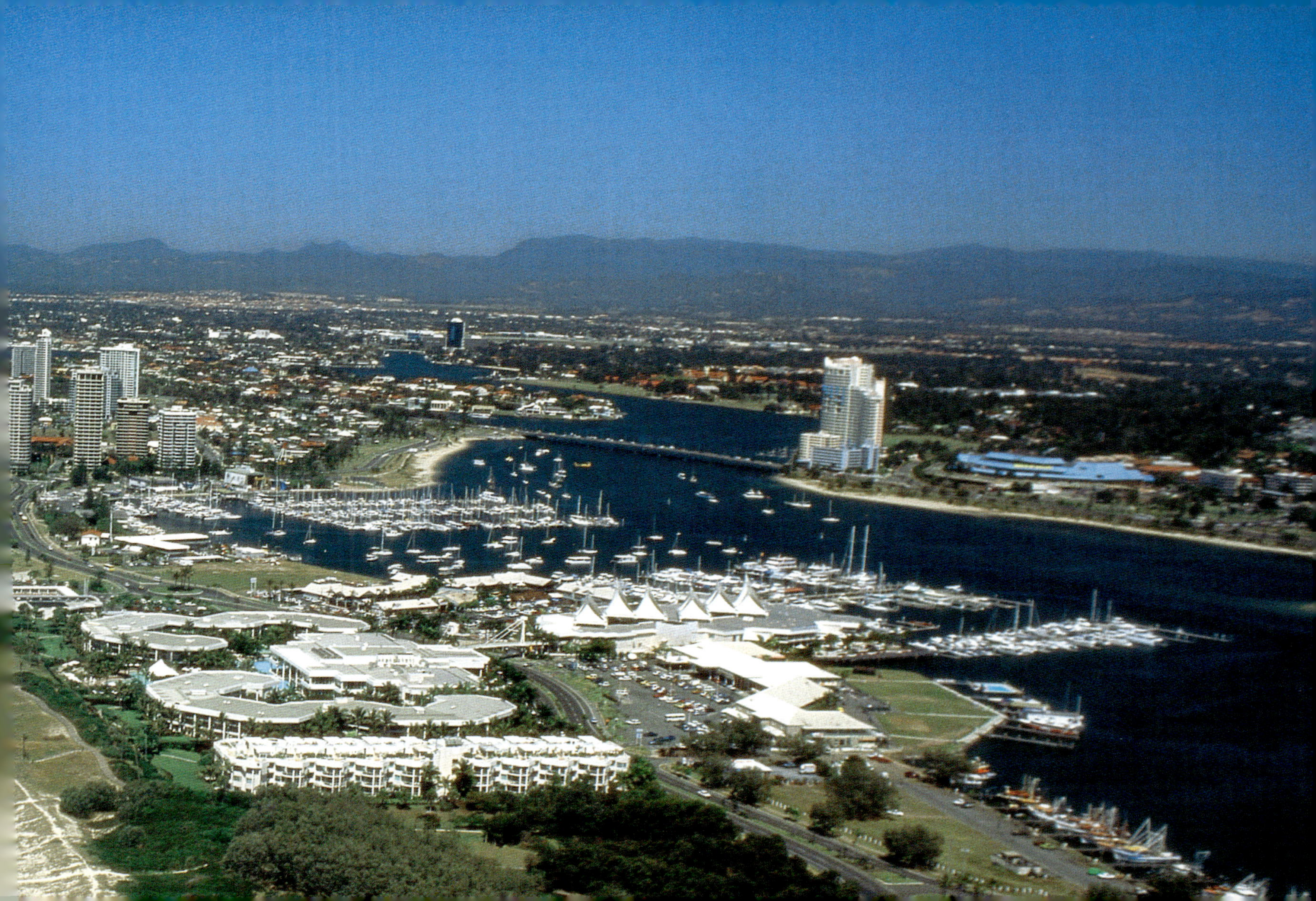

Eastern grey kangaroo.

King parrot at Currumbin Wildlife Sanctuary.

Emus are flightless birds second in height only to ostriches.

Koalas are often well disguised in the tops of eucalyptus trees.

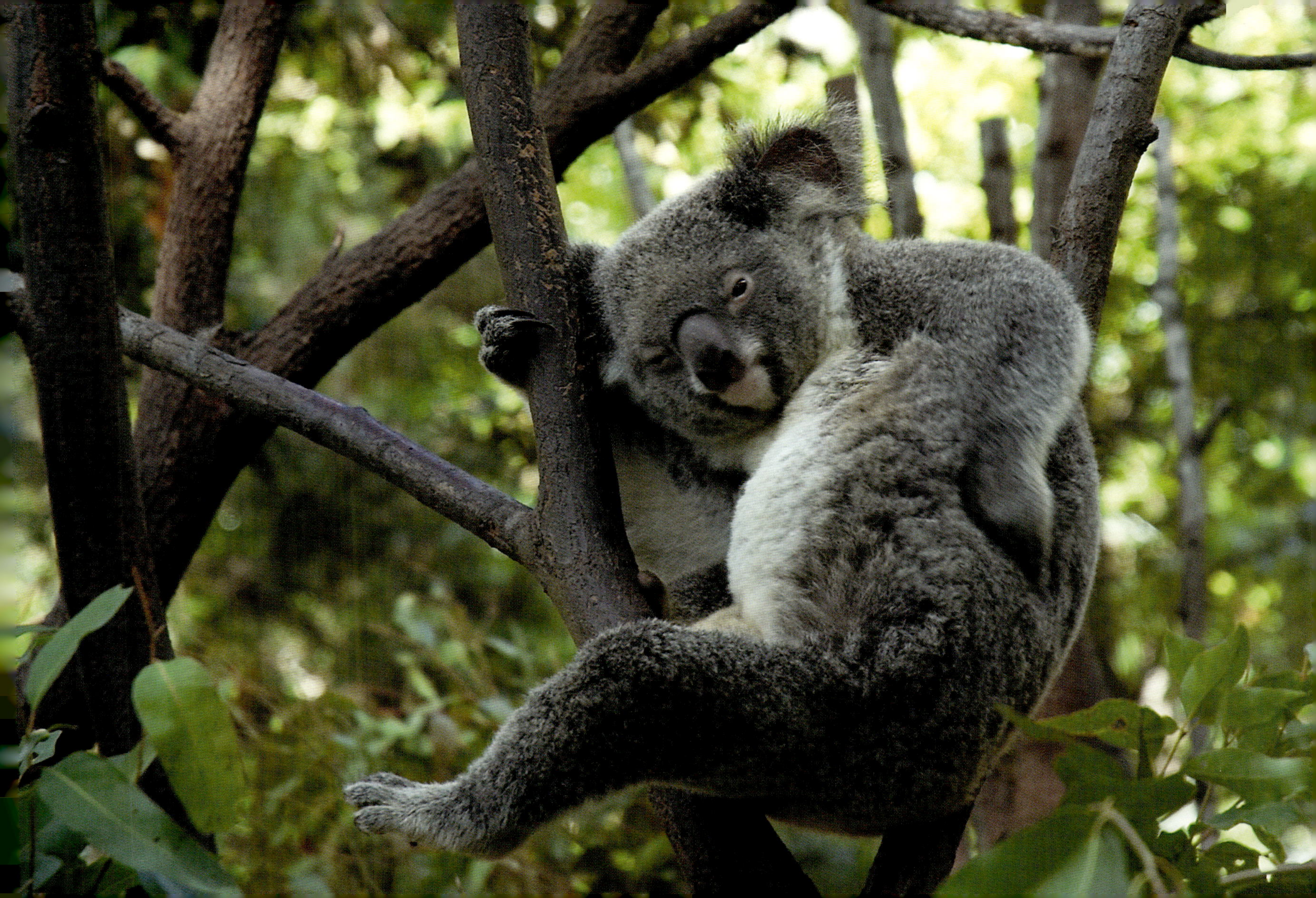

Surfing is a way of life on the Queensland beaches and as the sun rises over the horizon, the first enthusiasts head off in search of the perfect wave.

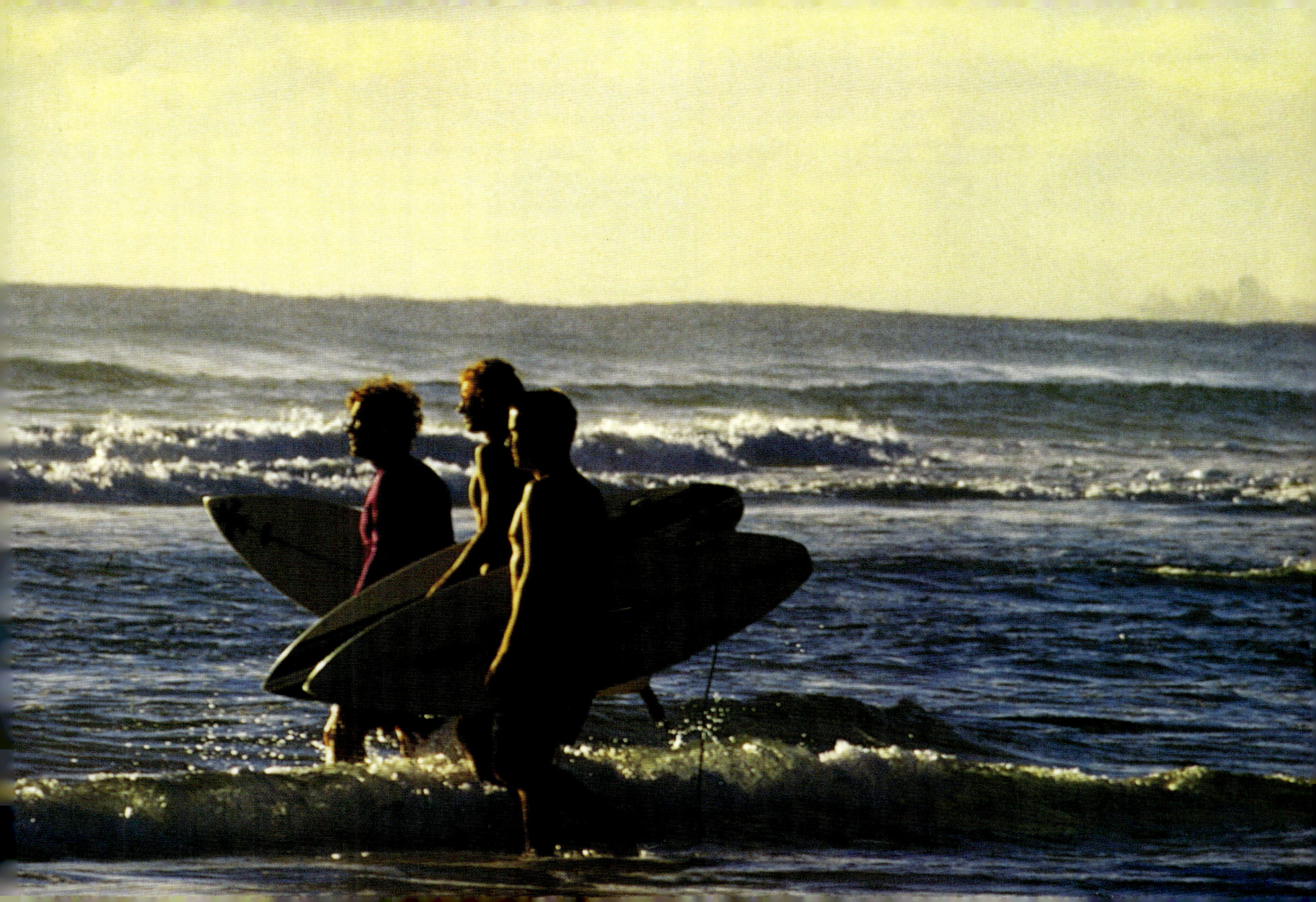

Above: The sparkling waters of the Great Barrier Reef invite snorkellers and divers to explore a wonderland of marine treasures.

Right: Heron Island, an important marine biology research site, is known for the diversity of its reef life as well as for the green turtles which come ashore every year to lay their eggs.

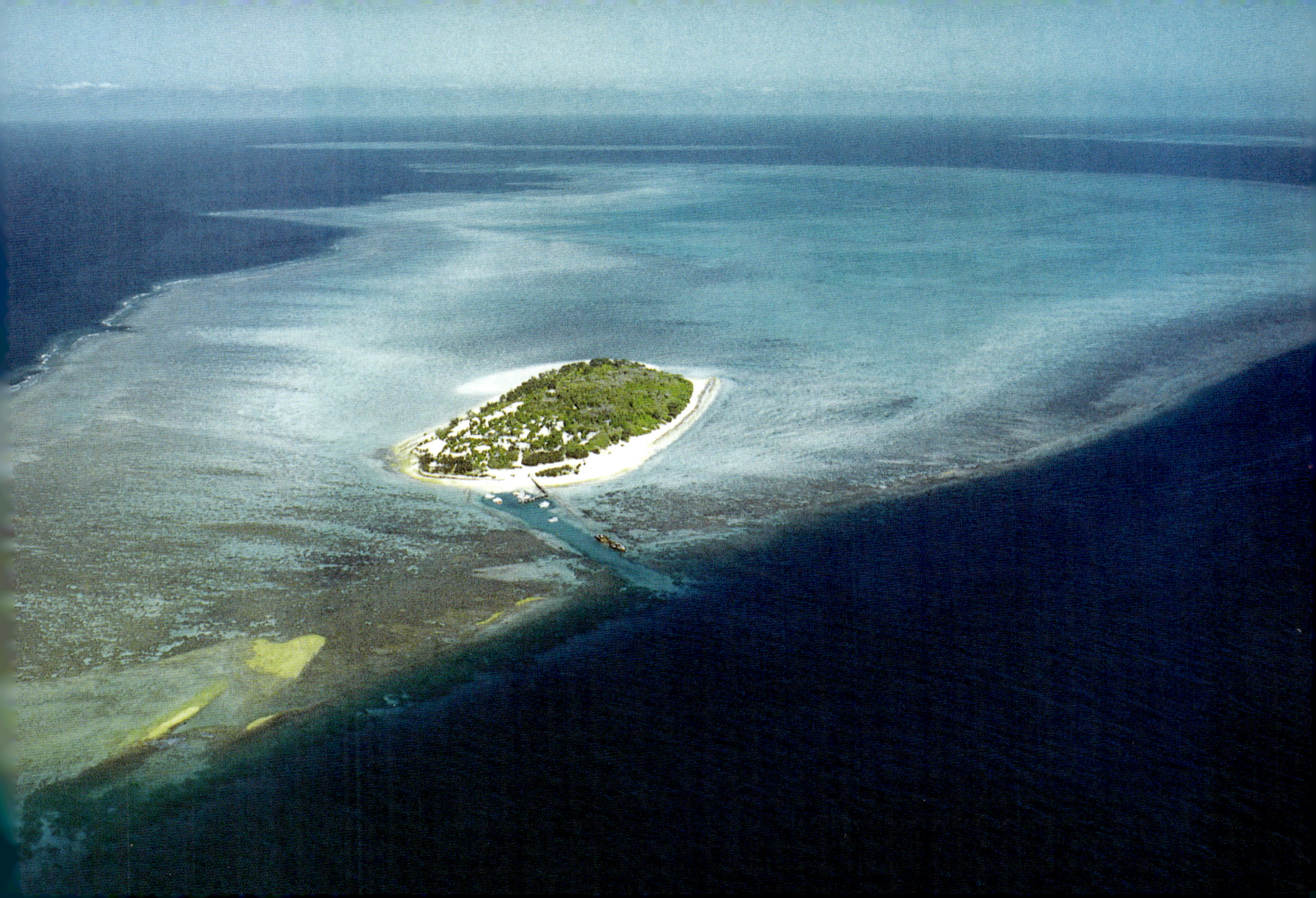

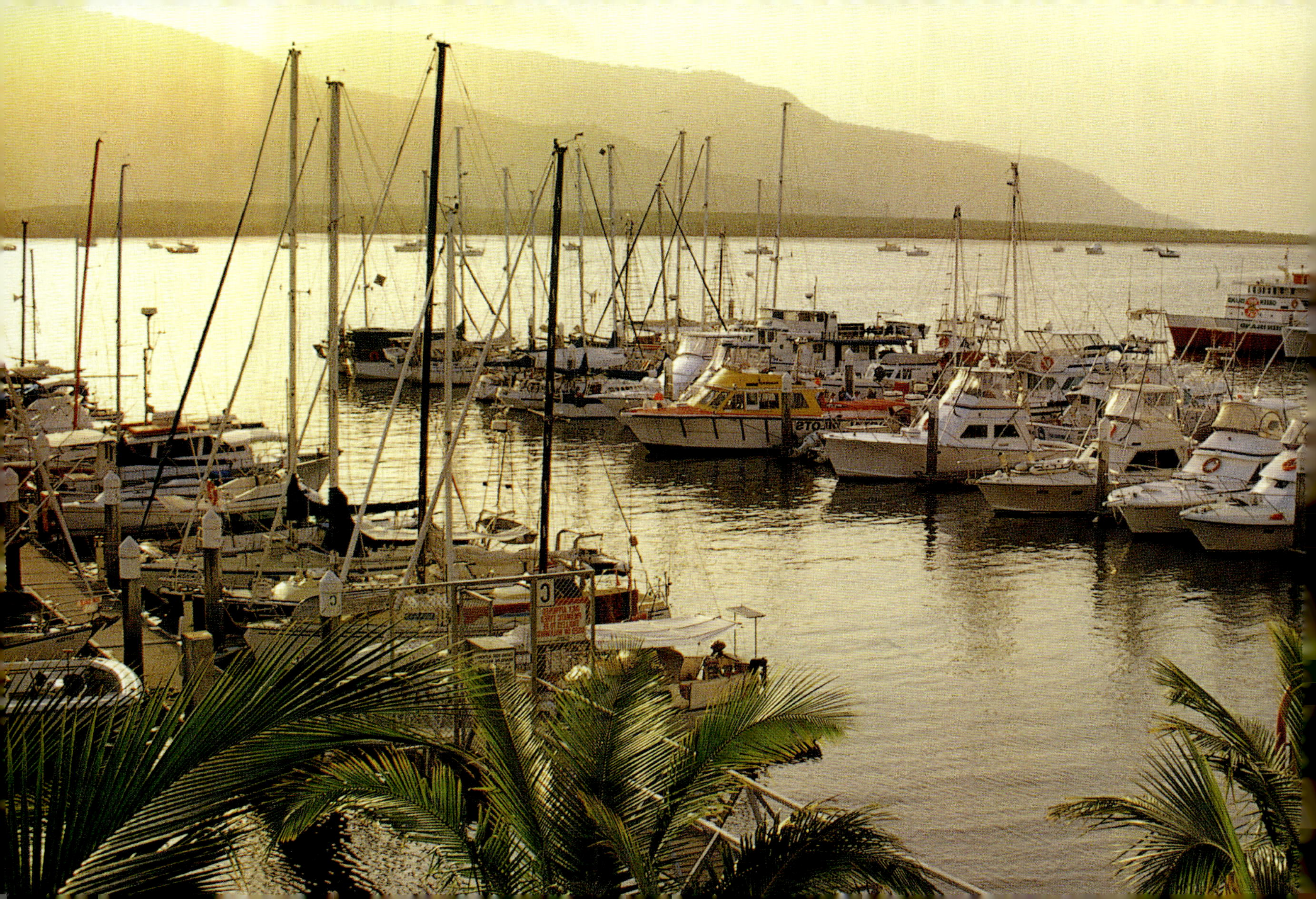

Above: Tjapukai Aboriginal Cultural Park introduces visitors to traditional Aboriginal life.

Top: A scenic railway runs between Cairns and the town of Kuranda on the Atherton Tablelands.

Left: The tropical town of Cairns is the departure point for many trips to the Great Barrier Reef.

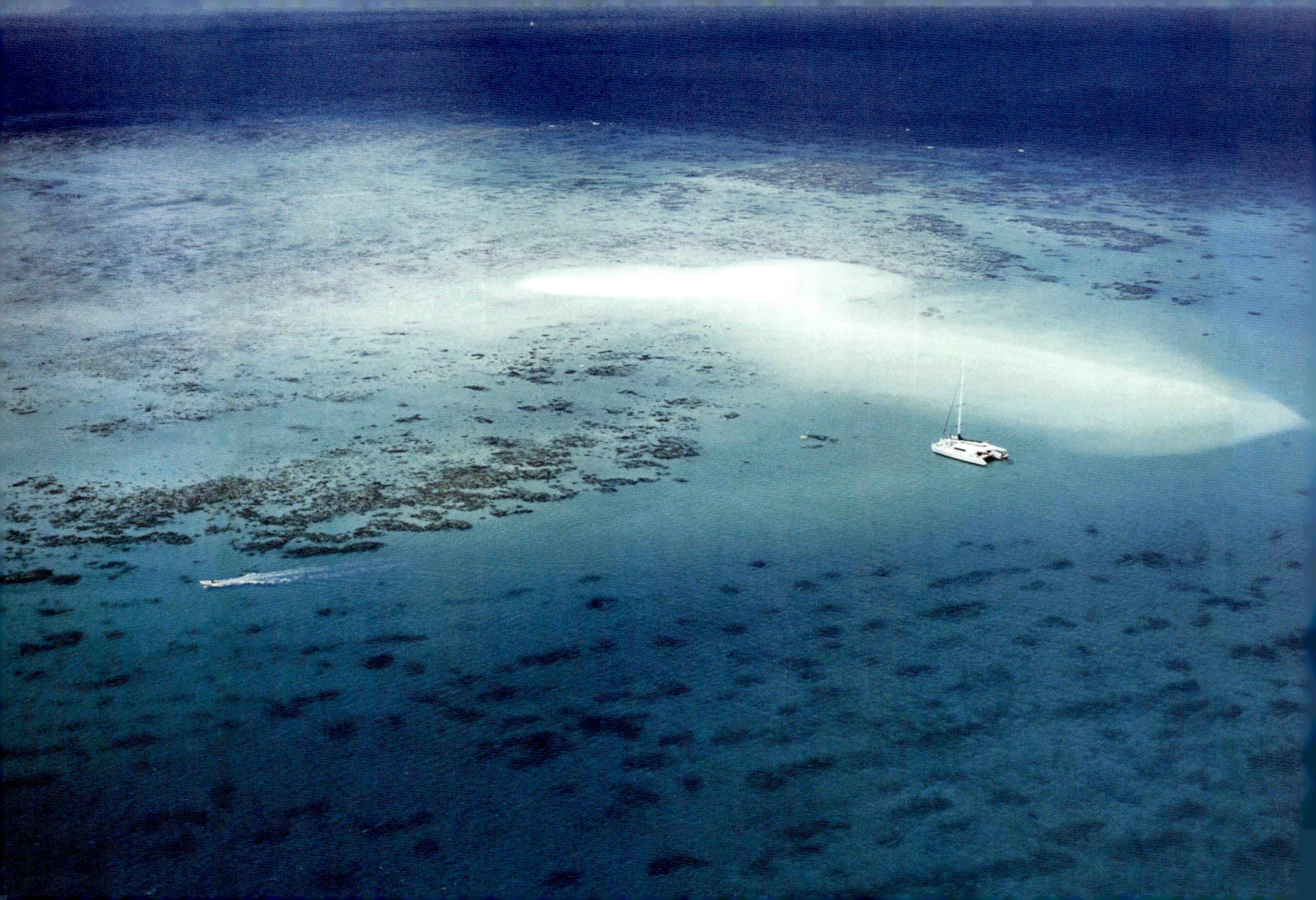

Above and left: The Great Barrier Reef covers more than 230,000 square kilometres and is a complex ecosystem of tiny sand cays, palm-fringed islands and over 2,000 separate reefs.

Snorkelling in the waters of the Great Barrier Reef.

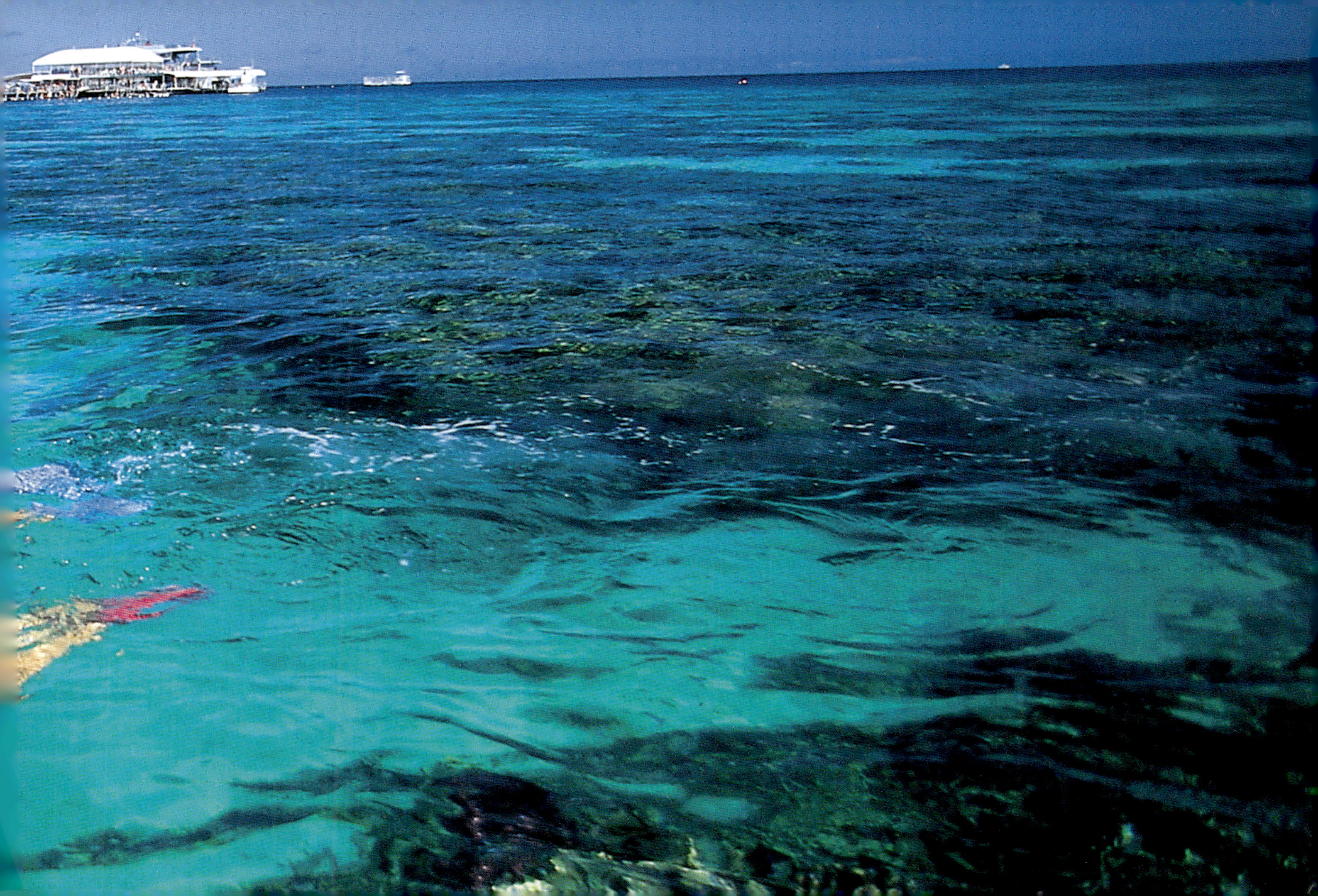

Queensland is a prime spot for divers.

Noosa Heads on the Sunshine Coast.

Above and right: To the north of Cairns lies the World Heritage area of Daintree National Park. Its lush tropical rainforest extends down to the ocean in places and provides a habitat for a rich diversity of flora and fauna, many species of which are unique to the region.

Rural Longreach is located in central Queensland.

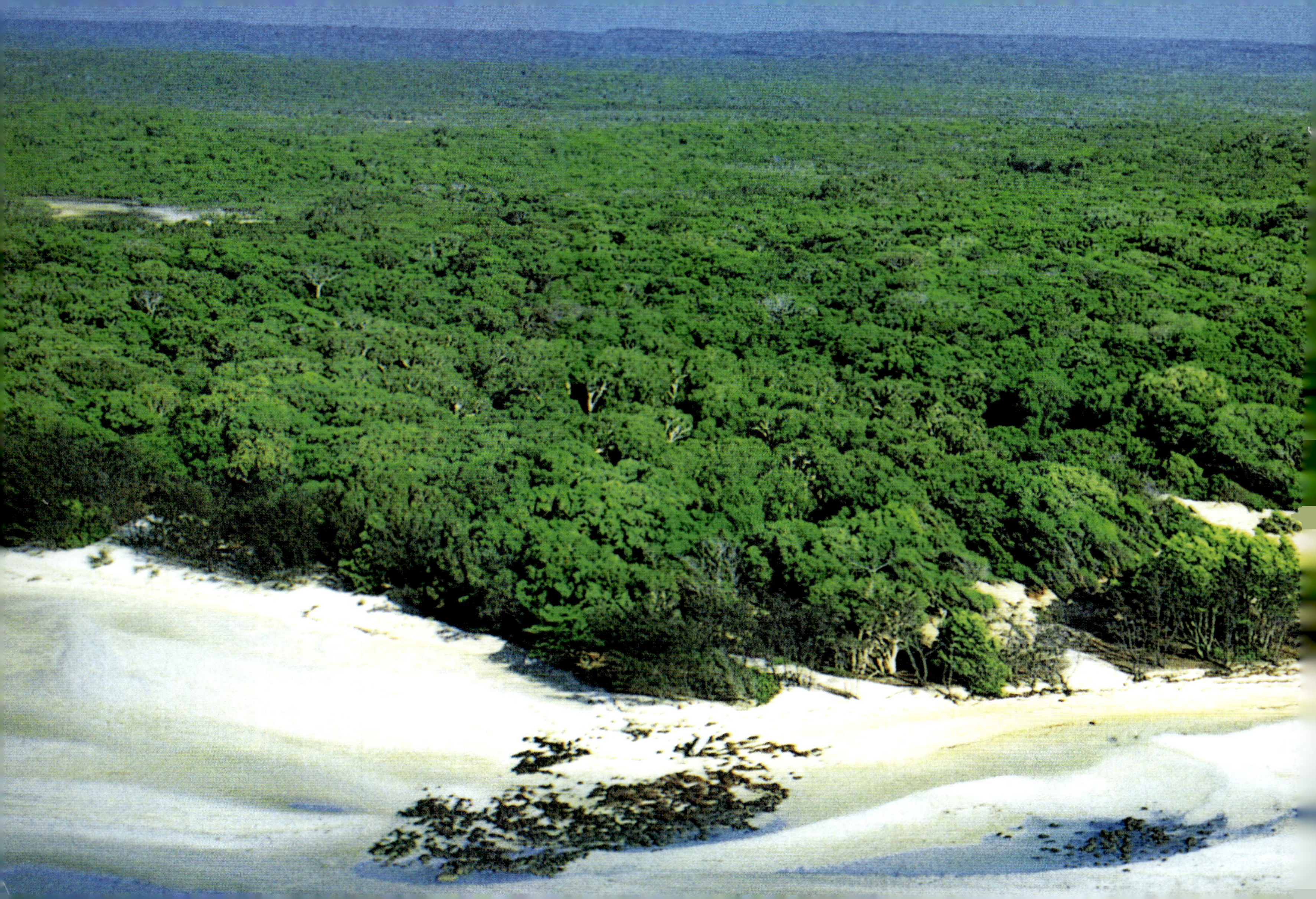

Cape York, the northernmost point of Queensland, has largely remained a region of untamed wilderness where desolate beaches and seemingly impenetrable mangrove forest recall a time before European settlement.